The Definitive Confucius:
A New Translation of *The Analects*

The Definitive Confucius:
A New Translation of *The Analects*

Translated from the Chinese by Wusun Lin

Long River Press
San Francisco

Published in the United States of America by
Sinomedia International Group
Long River Press
360 Swift Ave., Suite 48
South San Francisco, CA 94080

Cover design: Tiffany Cha
Text design: Linda Ronan

Library of Congress Cataloging-in-Publication Data

Confucius.
[Lun yu. English]
The definitive Confucius : a new translation of the analects / translated from the Chinese by Wusun Lin.
     pages cm
  Summary: "This new translation of the Concfucian Analects (Lunyu), the key book in Confucian studies. Professor Lin Wusun, one of China's foremost translators, has prepared this exhaustively researched version which will be regarded as the new standard"— Provided by publisher.
  ISBN 978-1-59265-127-6 (pbk.)
  I. Lin, Wusun, translator. II. Title.
  PL2478.L8 2012
  181'.112—dc23
                              2012033502

Printed in the United States of America

Contents

Preface

The Analects (also known as Lunyü) is the classic text on Confucius' teachings and experiences, was compiled by his disciples and second-generation disciples during the Spring and Autumn Period (722—480BC) in Chinese history. It is comprised of 20 separate "books", which are broken down into 492 passages. Though many of the passages are short, they often carry profound meaning.

For more than two thousand years, *The Analects* and Confucian thought have had an immeasurable impact on the Chinese people and Chinese culture. Confucian tradition constitutes the core and bedrock of the Chinese civilization, consistently making an impact on the development of China throughout history.

Though Chinese students today no longer recite the *Four Books* and *Five Classics*, Confucian thought is still subtly influencing the ethos of the Chinese people. Confucianism is still very much alive with its positive values concerning society and ethics.

Centuries ago, missionaries who had been to China began to introduce *The Analects* to the West. With China's increasing influence abroad, *The Analects* and Confucius have evoked widespread interest in the world. Confucius and Confucianism belong not only to China but also to the entire world.

Wusun Lin started the translation of *The Analects* in the late 1990s. Since then, he has read extensively Chinese and foreign books on *The Analects* as well as the latest studies in the field. Time and again, he revised his translation. To help readers better understand *The Analects* and Confucian thought, he included in the book accounts about the life of Confucius, the development of Confucian thought, and the lasting influence of Confucius on Chinese philosophy and society. Mr. Lin also added necessary background information and explanatory notes to important passages and terminologies found in *The Analects*. In addition, to further help Western readers, Mr. Lin draws comparisons between Confucius, Socrates, and even Jesus, in their thoughts, experiences and influences.

This new translation of *The Analects* by Mr. Lin will satisfy the needs of readers in understanding Confucian thought and Chinese culture. It is hoped that every notable quotation from the book will resonate with the reader and help him appreciate the intricacies and practicality of Chinese philosophy.

Introduction

Who was Confucius?

Confucius[1] (551—491 BC) ranks the foremost among China's ancient thinkers. His teachings had a profound influence on the development of Chinese history and left a deep imprint on the Chinese psyche. He is also said to have initiated private tutoring, which constituted a forward step in Chinese education. Prior to him, there existed only official schools, the sole preserves of the children of the aristocracy. People nowadays who are used to public education might not appreciate the full impact of private tutoring as a revolutionary measure which helped to promote social mobility in ancient China. The introduction of the system of imperial examination whose content, during most periods in Chinese history, centered on Confucius' teachings, gave the children of different social background, particularly the under-privileged, a chance to pass the examination and move up the social ladder. To commemorate the Master, Confucius temples existed all over China, even down to the counties, the country's basic administrative unit.

Confucius was born during what is known as the Spring and Autumn Period (722-480 BC) in Chinese history. His native state

---

1. *Latinized version of Kong Fuzi (Master Kong). His full name is Kong Qiu (孔丘).

was Lu, located in what is now Shandong Province in eastern China. At that time, the Zhou Dynasty (1030-211 BC) was in serious decline. Its rule was confined to a limited domain. The heads of its vassal states, whose rulers were mostly descendents of the first king's close relatives and ministers, simply went their own way. And these vassal states were fighting among themselves, sometimes to the extent of the stronger conquering the weaker ones. Within these states, ministers often turned their rulers into puppets. Usurpations and palace coups were commonplace. It was in these tumultuous times that Confucius grew up. He therefore turned to the past to seek inspiration and role-models and to find cures and solutions to current social ills. Many of the ancient concepts were developed and heroes reconstructed to fit in with Confucius' own philosophical and ethical ideas. And he called on the young to surpass the old. In this sense, he may be considered a traditionalist, but not a conservative.

Confucius had a unique childhood. His father Shuliang Ge[2] was a warrior of rather low status. Generations back, one of his forefathers, a distinguished aristocrat by the name of Kong Fujia, had moved to the state of Lu from the neighboring state of Song to escape persecution after a palace coup there. His mother was his father's third wife. Already in his 60s, Shuliang Ge had married her, a young woman from the capital, Qufu, in the hope that she would bear him a healthy son. She accomplished that, only to see her husband die when Confucius was only three. She then moved back home with her son and, despite a difficult life, devoted her entire energy to bringing up the child with distinction. Confucius did not fail his mother's expectations. His low social status did not prevent him from mastering the language skills, history and other branches of knowledge. A self-taught man, he took up various lowly jobs and avidly studied all the historical documents he could lay hands on. He thus became a widely-recognized scholar.

In this capacity, he began to teach while looking for official posts by offering advice to the rulers and high officials of Lu. Despite several failures, he did once become a senior official himself. However, when he tried to introduce reforms in accordance with his political

2. Kong is his surname while Shuliang is his style name and Ge his assumed name.

doctrines, he met with strong resistance as these moves affected the vested interests of the officialdom. According to tradition, Confucius was appointed the Minister of Justice, but the duke of Lu and his chief minister stopped attending court when the neighboring state of Qi presented them with a troupe of singsong girls to distract them from Confucius' reform programs. He therefore decided to seek his political future abroad. He traveled to many states with his disciples and offered his service to their rulers. He was received with honor in several of the states. However, none took his advice seriously. Totally disappointed, he returned to Lu 13 years afterwards and spent the rest of his life teaching and editing ancient classics. His health impaired by the untimely death of his son and two of his most beloved disciples, he died at the age of 73, still convinced that he had a historic mission.

The Analects and Confucius' Ideas

The Analects, probably compiled after Confucius' death by his disciples and disciples' disciples who put their heads together to recollect what the Master had said and done, was originally in the form of wooden or bamboo strips. These were destroyed by order of Qin Shi Huang, the first emperor of the Qin Dynasty (221-206 BC), who was a believer in legalism and authoritarian rule. Confucian scholars and texts perished in large numbers in his notorious campaign of extermination. Not long after, during the early Han Dynasty (206BC-220AD), Emperor Wudi adopted the Confucian doctrines at the advice of his minister, the scholar Dong Zhongshu, a move which contributed to the stability of his rule. From then on, Confucian ideas won the favor of the ruling class and therefore enjoyed a privileged position in China. As time went by, Confucius was idolized as a sage and Confucianism became the dominant thought.

However, owing to Qin Shi Huang's persecution, only three versions of *The Analects* survived. There was an edition in the State of Lu, and another in the neighboring Qi. Soon, another was discovered, hidden in the wall of the house of Confucius' descendents. *The Analects* we have today is an edited version which has probably experienced many changes through the ages. This can be proved as new versions of the classic have been found in ancient tombs by archeologists in recent years.

Confucius' overriding concern was the formation of a good government. To make this possible, he envisaged a virtuous and wise ruler who cared for his people and whose own meritorious behavior would make him a role model for his ministers and subjects. He would surround himself with virtuous ministers and distance himself from unscrupulous servitors. At the bottom level, Confucius devised the formation of a harmonious family which he considered the nucleus of the society. There was a whole set of rules guiding the hierarchical relationship between father and sons, between husband and wife, between elder and younger brothers and between friends. Trust, mutual concern and the sense of right and wrong were considered much more important and effective in weaving the social fabric than the implementation of strict rules and regulations. Life-long learning and continuous strivings to improve one's ethical standard would make one a man of honor worthy of admiration and emulation. That, he believed, would contribute to the making of an ideal society. A passage in *The Great Learning,* another Confucian classic taken from the ancient document *Li Ji* and edited by the Song Dynasty Confucian scholar, Zhu Xi (1130-1200), best epitomizes the above Confucian ethical-political ideal when it stated: Cultivate yourself and then your family will be put in order. When all the families achieve that, then the local government will be well run, and that will lead to peace and order in the whole country.

To us moderns, Confucius was not free of mistaken and outdated ideas. His belittlement of women is notorious. Some current scholars tried to explain away his saying in this regard by giving us a different interpretation. However, this is not really necessary when we remember that Confucius lived in a patriarchal society where women had no social status and Confucius' attitude was merely a reflection of his times. Another passage showed him to consider the common people to be too ignorant so that there was no need for one to bother with informing them of what was going on. Still another such anachronism was his low opinion of physical labor such as farming and gardening. When his disciple Fan Chi asked him about his view on these matters, he answered he knew nothing about them, adding later that Fan Chi was indeed a petty man. The whole question hinges on how we should look at positive historical figures. However great they might be, they should not be put on a pedestal, prettified or glorified beyond their true selves. Confucius was what he was, a great thinker despite all his faults.

In *The Analects*, we find Confucius a very human figure, with his likes and dislikes, his hopes and disappointments, sometimes even a bit self-contradictory in his sayings. Confucius was convinced he had a great historic mission, given him by heavenly mandate. Yet he was so often disappointed that he sometimes lamented he was little understood. Once he exclaimed that he was going to go overseas on a raft. On another occasion he said it was not a bad idea to live among the tribal people.

After Confucius' death, his disciples dispersed to different states to spread his ideas, establishing various schools of thought themselves. Both Mencius and Xunzi were distinguished masters during the following Warring States period (475-221 BC). As time went by, there were different interpretations of Confucian ideas and this process has lasted ever since.

Confucius, Socrates and Jesus

For Western readers to fully appreciate Confucius, it is perhaps useful to touch on the commonalities as well as the differences between him and two leading lights of Western thought, i.e., Socrates and Jesus.

1. All three lived at times of crisis.

2. Both Confucius and Socrates (469-399 BC) lived in times which some Western historians called the Axial Age, when humankind began to ask some ultimate questions about life and the universe, about knowledge, truth and justice. Jesus came later, but he dealt with God and afterlife, and about the coming of the heavenly kingdom. Confucius, on the other hand, was a this-worldly thinker. Though he did believe in Heaven, destiny and the like, he avoided such subjects as the gods and supernatural forces. When asked about death, he answered that since we did not know enough about life, why should we bother about death and what happens afterwards. He never touched on what the Western people call ultimate ques-

tions like where we come from and where we are heading, or about afterlife. This characteristic of his mindset had a deep influence on the Chinese people.

3. All three were not appreciated while they lived and all three faced severe tests. Socrates was charged with the corruption of the Athenian youth and sentenced by the city court. He chose to drink hemlock instead of being exiled. Jesus was crucified. Confucius died a natural death though he was never really given a chance to fulfill his self–determined mission.

4. All three became influential, thanks to the "missionary work" of their disciples and their ideas have since influenced the course of history. Confucius' ethical and political ideas, Socrates' analytical method aimed at probing the issues by dialogue and Jesus' compassion and his monotheism all became the most precious of the world's spiritual and cultural heritage.

5. In some ways, *The Analects* mean to the Chinese people before the end of the imperial dynasties in 1911 what the Bible means to the Western world. One, it has left a deep imprint on the Chinese mindset, just as the Bible has on its readers in the West. Two, some similar ideas are expressed. For example, in the New Testament (Matthew) it says "Do unto others what you want them to do unto you". In *The Analects*, there is "Don't do unto others what you would not want others to do unto you", now known as the Golden Rule. Three, just as the Bible influenced the Western languages, *The Analects* enriched the Chinese language with many of its sayings and anecdotes, many of which are still very popular in daily use and in literary works. Four, tens of thousands of interpretations and annotations by scholars through the ages have been written about both works.

What was there in Confucius and his doctrines that made them so important?

To Confucius, politics and ethics formed an integral whole. He emphasized that one had first to learn how to improve himself and his relationship with others before he could run the government well. He therefore considered self-improvement a life-long process. To him, learning is not only limited to acquiring knowledge. It is mainly for upgrading one's own moral fiber and becoming a true man of honor.

However, it would be a mistake to consider Confucian ideas the sole trend of thought in traditional China. After Confucius' time and during the Warring States Period, there were many different schools of thought, such as those advocated by Laozi (Daoism, also translated as Taoism), Mozi (Moism) and Han Feizi (Legalism). In fact, there have been so many of them that it was described as a period where "a hundred schools of thought contend." At least a dozen of them were prominent. Later, Confucianism, Buddhism and Daoism (Taoism) came to the fore and they gradually achieved coexistence. However, throughout Chinese history, there were criticisms of Confucianism and some of these challenges represented brilliant gems in the history of ideas. And this was especially true during periods of turbulence.

The influence of Confucianism was not limited to China alone. For thousands of years, throughout East Asia, especially in Korea, Japan and Viet Nam, it enjoyed widespread recognition and today its impact on the local culture and politics can still be felt. This is especially noticeable in the island state of Singapore.

In modern China, when the country suffered severe defeats and setbacks at the hands of Western invaders, Chinese people, first of all the intellectuals, gradually came to the conclusion that something was seriously wrong with the country's basic political system, culture and ideology. That was the background to the May 4th New Cultural Movement of 1919 when democracy and science were introduced to the country and the slogan "Down with the Confucian Shop" was raised. It was a battle between the progressives, who wanted to introduce to China advanced Western ideas and systems to move the country ahead, and the conservatives, who wanted to keep China as it was. Confucianism was used by the latter as a rod to beat down the new radicals.

During modern Chinese history, there existed two camps on Confucius—pros and cons. Lu Xun, the influential modern progressive writer, and noted stateswoman Soong Ching Ling (Madame Sun Yat-sen) were both very critical of Confucius. Mao Zedong, on the other hand, once wrote that "We should sum up our history from Confucius to Sun Yat-sen and take over this valuable legacy."

The second time Confucius suffered a concerted attack was during the "Cultural Revolution" (1966-1976), but since the criticism was so far-fetched and the true target of the campaign was some current political figures, it soon became a farce.

While Confucius was left alone in the years following the "Cultural Revolution", he soon became a subject of theoretical interest among scholars. The first serious attempt to restore Confucius' place in history was made in the 1980s by Kuang Yaming, a scholar and then president of Nanjing University. This was soon followed by the establishment of the Confucius Research Institute. Today, more and more, objective study has come to the fore.

However, what has really raised scholars' eyebrows is the fact that there has now appeared a mounting, popular fervor for Confucius and *The Analects*. Not only have lectures on Confucius become a great draw among university students, books on the subject have been published in hundreds of thousands of copies. A woman professor by the name of Yu Dan gave a series of TV lectures on Confucius and *The Analects*. This was followed by the publication of her book on the same topic. Both achieved phenomenal success. She was invited to speak in numerous cities, including Taipei, Seoul and Tokyo, and even in England. Meanwhile, other scholarly and popular books about Confucius and his teachings continue to hold the public's attention. A full-length feature film on Confucius directed by the famous woman director Hu Mei is being produced and is scheduled to be released in the near future. And a TV series about the Master is also under preparation. All signs show that the fervor for Confucius will rise still further. And it is interesting to note that China has established nearly 300 Confucius Institutes in 87 countries around the world within a few years, both to teach the Chinese language and Chinese culture. Internationally, too, there have been many new translations of *The Analects* and the study of Confucianism has made notable advances.

How can we explain Confucius' renewed popularity in China? It can be found in an analysis of several factors.

Firstly, if anything, the "Cultural Revolution" proved by negative example that tradition cannot be destroyed either by diktat or by mass movement and that cultural values have a great staying power.

In other words, it proved that the present, culturally as well as ideologically, can only be developed on the basis of the past, by sublimation rather than any other simplistic method. Secondly, now, 30 years after China's reform and opening up, the material well-being of most of its people has more or less been satisfied. What they need is some kind of political, spiritual and intellectual satisfaction. They need to find their cultural identity. In other words, the more prosperous the country becomes, the more people look for political, social, and cultural satisfactions. And for this they need a new culture in line with the best of China's traditions. Simultaneously, the more prosperous and powerful China becomes, the greater its people's interest in the country's past. Along with the flood of post-modern pop cultures which has inundated the Chinese market, there is also a return to the country's cultural traditions. This has been amply demonstrated by renewed academic and popular interest in the past, the restoration of traditional holidays, and renewal of a good number of Chinese intangible cultural heritages and of the country's many ethnic groups. Studies of and attention to the Great Wall, the Terracotta soldiers, the Dunhuang Caves, the seven voyages (1405-1433) of Admiral Zheng Ho during the Ming Dynasty[3], for example, have also increased.

Let us cite an example of how the best of Confucian ideas is being developed to form one of China's basic state policies. The call for a harmonious society at home and a harmonious world can be traced back to Confucius' principles of "harmony is precious" (和为贵), "harmony but not sameness" (和而不同) and "a myriad things each following its own course without interfering with others" (道并行而不相悖). This policy has won widespread recognition because experience has proved that it serves the basic interests of people the world over.

Several questions need clarification before we proceed further.

One, Confucianism need not be mutually exclusive with regard to other philosophical theories and to religions. It has existed alongside Buddhism and Daoism for millennia. In fact, they even interpenetrated each other.

---

3. His voyages to Southeast Asia, India and Africa predate Columbus' voyages (1492-1498) by more than 50 years.

Today, many Chinese thinkers have absorbed the best of their teachings for their own benefit and for the service of the people.

Two, Confucianism, as an ethical theory, is unique, but when we study it closely, we find that it has many points in common with Christianity and other religions. Examples are legion. For example, you will find the different religions all have their own sayings about the Golden Rule, i.e., "Don't do unto others as you would not like others to do to you." So we can say that the different civilizations need not be mutually exclusive and can and need to coexist in our present inter-connected world, so close are they to each other that it has truly become a global village.

Three, in our age, while congratulating ourselves on our phenomenal advances, we are at the same time humbled by the reverses our humankind has experienced. More than ever we are painfully aware of the fact that our knowledge of the world, the universe and the cosmos is still very limited and that we still have a long way to go in our quest for truth. In both natural and social sciences, there are still many unexplored fields. In economics, as the present financial crisis has shown, we are still groping in the dark in some areas and on some matters, and no economy has proved to be faultless. It would be more intellectually honest and beneficial to be open-minded and try to draw from the best of the different theories and sublimate them.

Four, in China today, what we are witnessing throughout the 30 years of opening and reform is the attempt to draw the best from different theories and apply them according to Chinese conditions. The development of socialism and the advance in material wealth is accompanied by the stress on morality, the growth of religious beliefs and the throwback to tradition alongside the intake of Western ideas. Western and traditional Chinese medicine (TCM), Western classical music and ballet alongside Chinese traditional music, Peking Opera and a variety of local operas, Chinese cuisine of all sorts and international cuisines all have their place in China, to cite only a few examples. Life, as in the case of Nature, becomes multifarious and colorful. So also the world's development approaches and social systems. There is no single universal model. While there do exist universal values, their application depends very much on the uniqueness of each local situation, the differing social and historical situation in different parts of the world. The great commonality which Confucius spoke of and which was expounded by the scholar Kang Youwei of the late Qing Dynasty and the early Republic as well as Dr. Sun Yat-sen, the founding father of the Chinese Republic, is a vision which nobody knows when it will materialize.

What can readers from abroad who are interested in China learn from *The Analects*? Young readers may enrich their knowledge and vision by reading this ancient classic. They will find Confucius a friend who crossed the time channel to provide them with much worldly wisdom. Those interested in Chinese culture and plan to work in China will find in it useful tips to Chinese people's values, such as the stress on family and on human relationships, respect for the elderly and the great attachment to learning and moral self-improvement. This latter is significant since the majority of the Chinese people are not religious believers, yet there is amongst them a strong sense of right and wrong inherited from their early family influence and school education where, if we look close enough, we can still find some pervading influence of Confucian thought.

Here we might offer a bit of advice: Like with all classics, *The Analects* is best read with a historical perspective. The current world, both in China and in other parts of the globe, is so different from the times of Confucius. There are components of his teaching which are outdated. But some of his ideas still carry great weight when we look into their deeper meanings. In other words, make use of *The Analects* as is applicable to your own situation. And you will benefit greatly from your encounter with Confucius.

Confucius' Disciples

Since a good number of the passages in *The Analects* are in the form of dialogue between Confucius and his disciples, it is important to familiarize our readers with the names and character of some of the disciples.

Tradition has it that during his lifetime, Confucius had 3,000 disciples, of whom 72 were the most prominent. That may be an exaggeration as the Master took students regardless of their social status. He did not run a school as we understand the term today. He either led them in discussions or answered their questions individually. Some scholars claim that "his disciples" included his disciples' disciples. If that was so, then the figure 3,000 might be justified. Whatever the case, among the 72 disciples, only 29 were mentioned in *The Analects*.

Before we list them, we need to explain how Chinese names, especially those ancient names, are formed.

1, Chinese names are confusing to English-language speakers for more than one reason. First of all, the Chinese surname comes before the given name.

2, Up till modern times, literate Chinese often had more than one name. Besides his surname and given name, he had a styled name (字*zi*), which his friends often used when talking or referring to him, and several assumed names (号*hao*). For example, Zilu (子路), one of Confucius' leading disciples, is known in *The Analects* as 1) Zhong You (仲由), which is his real name, 2) You (由), 3) Zilu (子路) and 4) Jilu (季路) ,"Ji" denoting that he was the fourth son in the family. To simplify matters, we have stuck to one name for each person in the translation.

In the following listing, we will give a brief description of a few of Confucius' disciples. This will help show the different relationship the Master had with his disciples, and also give some insight on why Confucius sometimes expressed different ideas on the same subject. The Master picked his words and explanations according to the level of understanding of his disciples. For example, he gave different answers to different disciples when asked the same question of what the term "humaneness" meant.

1, Yan Hui (颜回) was the Master's most favorite disciple. Extremely poor but very studious, he followed Confucius' lessons carefully and with whom he never had any disagreement. His early death certainly affected his influence in the spread of the Master's teaching.

2, Zilu (子路) was in many ways the opposite of Yan Hui. He was eager to express his views in front of the Master, He was outspoken, straight-forward, not afraid to express different views and even criticized Confucius despite his loyalty. He was courageous even to the point of rashness. Zilu died in battle while still middle-aged. He was a heroic figure, but he, too, had little influence in propagating Confucius' ideas.

3, Zigong (子贡) was perhaps the most eloquent of the Master's disciples. Unlike Yan Hui, he came from a prosperous family background. He took up office several times and distinguished himself by his business acumen.

4, Zeng Cen (曾参) was known as Master Zeng to Confucius' second-generation disciples. He stressed the importance of filial piety and had great influence in the spread of Confucian thought.

5, Zixia (子夏), like Zeng Cen, was one of Confucius' younger disciples. He was eloquent and noted for his literary achievements. After the Master's death, he, along with Zigong and Zeng Cen, played a leading role in spreading Confucius' teachings.

6, Ranyou (冉由) looked very much like Confucius and even once pretended to be his Master, only to be exposed when he could not answer his fellow disciples' questions. After Confucius' death, he was among those disciples who tried to make Confucius a sage, although the Master never claimed to be one.

Yan Hui, Zeng Cen and Ranyou were the Master's favorites because they were quick in understanding his ideas and their implications, few in words, careful in action. In short, different yet, nonetheless, future models of a man of honor.

Terminology in *The Analects*

In *The Analects*, Confucius employed a good number of terms to express his ideas on what were good ethics and politics. Many of these terms appeared in earlier classics, like *The Book of Songs, Yi Ching and Spring and Autumn*, but Confucius endowed them with new meanings. However, since Confucius only described but never defined them and since he gave different answers to the same terms depending on his disciples' individual characters and level of understanding, it is very difficult to find their exact definitions. Besides, as Classical Chinese is very concise and lends to different interpretations, there is no single English equivalent to these terms. For example, *ren* (仁) has been translated as benevolence, humanity, goodness, etc., *li* (礼) as rites and rituals, *junzi* (君子) as gentleman, exemplary person and *xiaoren* (小人) as petty man, common man and vulgar man. All this creates confusion and lends to different interpretations. Below I give my own renditions as well as the reasons for my choice. I hope they will help readers gain insight into Confucius' basic concepts and therefore his teachings.

1, *Junzi* (君子) literally means "son of the ruler", and therefore refers to a member of the aristocracy. In *The Analects*, the term was used by Confucius to describe his ideal person, the type who through self-improvement, becomes superior in ethics, gains peace of mind and therefore is fit to govern. To Confucius, people of low social ranks but willing to study and improve themselves can become *junzi*, whereas those scholars who are morally unfit cannot, thus giving the term strong ethical implications. *Junzi* has been translated as gentleman, but he is not the gentleman as used in today's English. In the present translation, I am using a "man of honor" to emphasize the difference and denote its ethical character.

2, *Xiaoren* (小人) literally means the common people, but Confucius used it mostly to refer to those who had petty interest in mind. In this translation, I am using "petty-minded people", and only occasionally "petty people" Here again, "petty-mindedness" has an ethical implication.

3, *Shi* (士) refers to the lowest echelon of the aristocracy. With their knowledge, they could become officials when they enjoyed the appreciation of the rulers. But then, the majority would retain their original status. Here I am following the traditional English rendition "scholar" to simplify matters.

4, *Ren* (仁) is rendered in this translation as humaneness. The simplest explanation Confucius gave to his disciple for this term was "To love others." The most famous quotation is "Don't do unto others what you don't want others to do unto you." Elsewhere, he stressed that what one wanted to achieve he should help others achieve too. However, Confucius did not advocate universal love.

5, *Li* (礼) was rather broad in content. It included rituals, etiquette, regulations and rules of proper behavior. During Confucius' time, there was no official law as we understand it today, but people would be punished when they violated the rules and regulations. Confucius paid great attention to *Li* which was set down when the Zhou Dynasty was first established. He believed that the neglect of *Li* was the cause of all troubles of his time. The ministers were neglecting it without any sense of shame, and their stewards and the society at large were following their examples. Confucius therefore considered it his mission to advise the powers-to-be to correct their ways through following *Ren* and restoring *Li*. The two concepts are closely related, the former being the kernel while the latter its outer form.

6, *Yue* (乐) is simply translated as music. In Confucius' time, there was a strict rule as to what kind of music was to be played in court, performed before visiting state leaders and on ceremonious occasions. It was therefore very important to handle it properly as it was considered to be a great booster of *Li*. Poems in *The Book of Songs*, China's most ancient collection of poetry, were often sung. Confucius was a great lover of music and often discussed with his disciples its intricacy and significance. Confucius considered it his task to teach the people *Li* and *Yue* which he believed would help people to achieve *Ren* and promote stability in society.

7, *Xiao* (孝) is filial piety. In the patriarchal society, the father had absolute power in the family, and the children's love and respect for him was considered very important. Related to this was the respect for the brothers, especially the eldest one, because he would take over the family after the father's death. This is called *Ti* (悌). Since the family, the basic unit of society, carried great weight during Confucius' time, he made *Xiao* and *Ti* basic ethical traits underpinning the society's stability, stressing that with them, no filial son would cause trouble and start a revolt against the state.

8, *De* (德) is virtue, still one of most popular terms in present-day China. Recently, the Chinese government has raised the slogan of building virtuous government (德政) to better run the country.

9, *Dao* (道) is usually rendered in English as "the Way". Its literal meaning is path or road, implying one need to master the true way of life and nature. It was widely used by ancient Chinese thinkers, the most well known to the West being (道德经) (*Daodejing*), or Tao Te Ching, also known as *Laozi*, and Sunzi's *The Art of War*.

10, *Yi* (义) has many different English translations, but the Chinese meaning is justice and righteousness, representing a kind of internal restraint. We have used both "justice" and "righteousness", depending on the context.

11, *Xin* (信) is rendered here as "trust", meaning "keep one's word in human relationship". "Trustworthy" is also used when the occasion requires.

12, *Tian* (天) It implies the master of Nature and humankind. And the emperors called themselves sons of heaven (天子). *Tian* does not have the meaning as in some religions where God lives and where good people go when they die. To simplify matters, we use heaven while reminding readers of the difference. In *The Analects*, the mandate of heaven is often used.

In conclusion, live the present, look to the future, but build on the past, that is a sure way to enrich one's life and achieve harmony within and without. That is the lesson I learnt reading and translating Confucius. I would like to pass it on to you our readers.

Book 1

Most books in *The Analects* do not have any central theme.

Book One, for example, meanders from topic to topic, the most prominent ones being learning (学*xue*), humaneness (仁*ren*), filial piety (孝*xiao*), the Way (道*dao*), righteousness (义*yi*) and rituals, etiquette, rules and regulations (礼*li*).

Besides Confucius, his disciples Zeng Cen and Ziyu were also called Masters, indicating that their sayings were also recorded by their disciples in the compilation. The prominent passages in Book One include 1.1, 1.4, 1.10, 1.14 and 1.16. Note that 1.1 and 1.16 both stress the importance of self-improvement, not recognition by others. That to Confucius is one of the marks of a man of honor.

1.1

The Master said, "Is it not a great pleasure to be able to practice frequently what you have learned? Is it not a real delight to have friends come to visit you from afar? Is it not the mark of a man of honor (君子*junzi*) to not take offence when others fail to appreciate your worth?"

1.2

Master You[1] said, "It is rare for one who is filial to his parents and respectful to his elder brothers to disobey his superiors. It is unheard of that one who would obey his superiors should go about creating trouble or even starting a rebellion. The man of honor devotes his attention to the basics. When he has mastered the basics, he is sure to find the key to the Way (道 *dao*). Couldn't we say that fulfilling one's filial and fraternal duties constitute the basics of being humane (仁 *ren*)?"

1.3

The Master said, "A smooth tongue and an ingratiating manner are seldom signs of being humane."

1.4

Master Zeng[2] said, "More than once do I examine myself everyday. Have I done my very best to help others? Have I been faithful to my friends? And have I practiced what my master has taught me?"

1.5

The Master said, "In governing a medium-sized state[3], one should devote himself whole-heartedly to state affairs, abide by his words, avoid excessive expenditure, care for his subordinates and use the labor of the common people (民 *min*) only during the slack season."[4]

---

1. You Ruo, Confucius' disciple.
2. Zeng Cen, Confucius' disciple.
3. The Chinese original was "a state equipped with a thousand chariots", equivalent to a medium-sized state during the Spring and Autumn Period.
4. Throughout ancient Chinese history, rulers had the right to call on the common people to work on public projects without recompense. The common people were mostly farmers. They had to work on the public projects, such as building defenses or digging canals without pay. If they had to fulfill these obligations during sowing or harvesting, their own farms would be neglected.

1.6

The Master said, "At home, a young man should be filial to his parents. Away from home, he should be respectful to his elders. He should be cautious and be true to his words. He should love his fellowmen and befriend the humane. If he still has energy to spare, let him devote himself to studying *wen*[5] (文).

1.7

Zixia[6] said, "When a man values virtue more than good looks , tries his best to serve his parents, is ready to sacrifice his life for his ruler and keeps his promises with his friends, then I say he is well-educated even if he has not had the benefit of being taught."

1.8

The Master said, "A man of honor would not have commanded respect if he lacked seriousness, and even if he had studied hard, his learning would not have a firm foundation. He pays great attention to loyalty and faithfulness and does not accept as friends those who don't follow the same moral principles. When he makes a mistake, he is not afraid of correcting himself."

1.9

Master Zeng said, "When funerals for parents are conducted strictly in accordance with the rituals (礼 *li*) and sacrifices to ancestors offered devoutly, then the morals of the common people will naturally thrive."

---

5. The study of historical documents and the six arts, i.e. rites, music, archery, charioting, writing and arithmetic.
6. Confucius' disciple.

1.10

Chen Kang[7] asked Zigong[8], "When our Master goes to another state, he is always able to learn a good deal about how it is governed. Does he go about seeking such information or do people there just give it to him of their own accord?"

Zigong answered, "Our Master gets the information he needs because he is temperate, kind, courteous, restrained and magnanimous. Our Master's way of gathering information is quite unique, isn't it?"

1.11

The Master said, "Observe a person's aspirations when his father is still around, then see how he behaves when his father has passed away. If three years later he still sticks to his father's way, he may be described as filial."[9]

1.12

Master You said, "In conducting the rituals, the principle of harmony is the most valuable. This was the most important aspect of the Way of the ancient kings. Everything they did, great or small, was done according to this rule. However, there is a limit to that. When harmony is sought for its own sake and when it is not regulated by rituals, then the principle will not work."

1.13

Master You said, "So long as a promise is in line with righteousness (义 yi), it should be kept. So long as respect conforms with rituals, it will keep humiliation at a distance. It follows that relying on those with whom one has close relationship[10] is dependable."

---

7. Confucius' disciple, also known as Ziqin.
8. Confucius' disciple, also known as Duanmu Ci.
9. The custom at Confucius' time required people to stay at home for three years after the death of their parents.
10. Here Ziyu was referring to one's relatives, both members of the same family or by marriage.

1.14

The Master said, "The man of honor seeks neither a full belly nor a comfortable house. He is quick in action, but cautious with his words. He corrects his own mistakes by learning from those who know the Way. He can thus be regarded as studious."

1.15

Zigong asked, "What do you think of one who is poor without being obsequious, wealthy without being arrogant?"

The Master answered, "That is pretty good, but not as good as one who is poor yet cheerful, or one who is wealthy yet observant of regulations and rituals."

Zigong said, "In the *Book of Songs*, there are these lines: 'As bone carved and polished, as jade cut and ground'. Is that what you meant?"

The Master said, "Oh, Zigong! Now I can discuss the *Book of Songs* with you. You know what is yet to come on the basis of what I have told you."

1.16

The Master said, "Do not worry about not being appreciated by others. Rather, worry about your not being able to appreciate them."

Book 2

Confucius stressed the importance of virtuous rule (德政 *dezheng*), and the need to indoctrinate the people with moral values as in 2.1 and 2.3 for the achievement of good governance. He was dubious of the effectiveness of harsh punishments alone. This was going to be the major difference between the Confucians and the legalists following Confucius' death. In 2.18, he talked about the need for an official to listen to different views and open his eyes to what was happening around him. And in 2.19 he emphasized the absolute necessity for the ruler to promote honest officials and distance himself from the dishonest ones. 2.4 is a very famous passage in which Confucius recalled the different stages of his personal history. It is often used as a guide to one's lifelong pursuit, or the way to maturity and success.

2.11, 2.15 and 2.17 provide insight into learning and knowledge. Reflection and recognition of the limit of one's knowledge are prerequisites for intellectual progress. In 2.5, 2.6, 2.7 and 2.8, Confucius returned to the subject of filial piety, another of his chief concerns.

2.1

The Master said, "He who rules the country by virtue can be compared to the Polestar which holds its own with a multitude of stars revolving around it."

2.2

The Master said, "The *Book of Songs* is made up of three hundred poems. They can be summed up in a single phrase, 'a pure heart saturated with unadulterated sentiments'."

2.3

The Master said, "Rule the people by decrees and put them into place by punishment and they will know how to stay out of trouble. But they will not have a sense of shame. Let them know the way of virtue and keep them in line with regulations and rituals, then they will not only have a sense of shame when they do wrong, but also know the correct course to take."

2.4

The Master said, "When I reached 15, I began devoting myself to learning. At 30, I could stand on my own. At 40, my mind was no longer confused. At 50, I knew what Heaven demanded of me. At 60, I was able to distinguish right from wrong in what other people told me. And since 70, I have been able to follow my heart's desire without transgressing the rules."

2.5

Meng Yizi[1] asked about filial piety. The Master answered, "Do not go against the rules."

Later, when Fan Chi[2] was driving a carriage for him, the Master said, "Meng Yizi asked what being filial meant and I answered, 'Do not go against the rules'."

"What did you mean by that?" asked Fan.

To which the Master answered, "When your parents are alive, serve them according to the rituals; when they pass away, bury and offer sacrifices to them according to the rituals, too."

---

1. A minister of the state of Lu.
2. Confucius' disciple.

2.6

Meng Wubo[3] asked about filial piety. The Master replied, "Let your parents have no cause for worry other than your health."

2.7

Ziyou asked about filial piety. The Master answered, "Nowadays, one is praised as a filial son because he is able to provide for his parents. However, he also provides for his dogs and horses. Where is the difference, then, if the son does not treat his parents with respect?"

2.8

Zixia asked about filial piety. The Master answered, "The difficulty lies in having the right feeling. Whether one consistently serves his parents with enthusiasm makes a big difference. If the son does nothing more than helping his parents when there is work to be done and sharing with them when food and drink are available, that alone can hardly be described as being filial."

2.9

The Master said, "Hui[4] never disagrees with me even when we spend the whole day talking to each other. It would seem as though he were slow-witted. But later I found that when he is on his own, he is quite creative. Hui is actually not slow-witted at all."

2.10

The Master said, "Observe a person's behavior, find out what leads him to behave the way he does and see what he rests content with. If one does that, how can that person still manage to hide his true character? How indeed?"

---

3. Son of Meng Yizi.
4. Yan Hui, Confucius' disciple.

2.11

The Master said, "He who is able to acquire new ideas while reviewing old knowledge is worthy of being a teacher."

2.12

The Master said, "A man of honor should not be a mere utensil."[5]

2.13

Zigong asked about the man of honor. The Master said, "He always puts his ideas into action before expressing them in words."

2.14

The Master said, "A man of honor associates with many but does not form a clique; the petty-minded man (小人 *xiaoren*) does the opposite."

2.15

The Master said, "Learning without reflection will end up in confusion; reflection without learning will end up in peril."

2.16

The Master said, "Attacking erroneous ideas will put an end to the harm they have caused."

2.17

The Master said, "Zilu[6], shall I tell you what true know-ledge is? Say you know when you know, and say you don't know when you don't, that is true knowledge."

---

5. A utensil serves only to fulfill one specific purpose. According to Confucius, a man of honor should be more than a specialist. He should be able to handle different tasks and situations. Compare this concept with the Renaissance man.
6. Confucius' disciple.

2.18

Zizhang[7] asked the Master how to be an official. The Master replied, "Listen to all kinds of opinions, set aside what is dubious and speak discreetly on the rest. That way, you will make few mistakes. Open your eyes wide, set aside what is dubious and act on the rest with caution. You will then have few regrets. Since a good official makes few mistakes, his success is ensured."

2.19

Duke Ai of the State of Lu asked, "What should I do so that my people will obey me?" The Master replied, "Your people will do so if you promote the straight over the crooked. They will disobey you if you do the opposite."

2.20

Ji Kangzi[8] asked, "What should be done to inculcate in the common people reverence and filial piety and eagerness to do their best?"

The Master replied, "Treat the common people with dignity, and they will treat you with reverence; promote filial piety and humaneness and they will be loyal to you; promote the righteous and instruct the incompetent, and they will eagerly do their best."

2.21

Asked why he had not become involved in government, the Master answered, "The *Book of Historical Documents* says, 'Piety means being filial to your parents and being fraternal to your brothers; spreading this idea will exert an influence upon the government.' If that is so, why must I take part in government?"

---

7. Confucius' disciple.
8. A minister of Lu.

2.22

The Master said, "How can a person get on if he is not trustworthy? It is just like a cart without a collar-bar or a carriage without a yoke-bar. How can he make it move?"

2.23

Zizhang asked, "Is it possible for us to know what it will be like ten generations from now?"

The Master answered, "It is possible to know the regulations and rituals which the Shang Dynasty inherited from the Xia Dynasty, including additions and omissions. In the same way, we come to know those which the Zhou Dynasty inherited from Shang. Therefore, should there be a successor to the Zhou Dynasty, it is also possible to know the regulations and rituals even a hundred generations from now."

2.24

The Master said, "It is servility to offer sacrifices to ancestors who are not one's own. It is cowardice not to uphold righteousness when it is called for."

Book 3

All the passages in Book Three are about rituals (礼 *li*), especially the close ties between rituals and music. They show the importance Confucius attached to this issue. He was very critical of the neglect and violations of age-old rules and rituals by the ministers of his time which he considered to be one of the chief reasons for the collapse of the Zhou Dynasty order.

3.1

The Master spoke thus of Jisun[1]. "He had eight rows of dancers perform for him in his courtyards. If this violation of the rituals can be tolerated, what cannot be?"

3.2

The three noble families of Lu had the *Yong* song[2] performed while their sacrificial offerings were being removed. The Master said, "It is said in the *Book of Songs* that 'With dukes in attendance, the Son of Heaven showed great solemnity when offering sacrifices.' How then is this song appropriate?"

---

1. One of the three families, namely Mengsun, Shusun and Jisun, who were then the most powerful nobles in the State of Lu.
2. A song reserved for royal occasions.

3.3

The Master said, "What have the rituals got to do with a person who is not humane? What have music and dance (乐 *yue*) got to do with him?"

3.4

Lin Fang[3] asked about the essence of the rituals. The Master answered, "What a good question that is! When performing a ritual, it is better to be frugal than to be extravagant. In mourning, it is more important to be really grief-stricken than to go through all the solemn formalities."

3.5

The Master said, "Even with a ruler, a culturally backward tribal state[4] is inferior to a state of the central plains without a ruler."

3.6

Jisun intended to offer sacrifices to Heaven on Mount Tai. On learning about this, the Master asked Ranyou[5], "Can't you stop him from doing that?" When Ranyou answered he couldn't, the Master said, "Alas, can it be that the God of Mount Tai knows less about the rituals than Lin Fang?"[6]

3.7

The Master said, "There is no contention between two men of honor. The only exception is perhaps archery. Even so, when the contest starts, the two archers bow to make way for each other. And when

---

3. Confucius' disciple.
4. Referring to those in the border areas.
5. Confucius' disciple.
6. Lin Fang knew the rituals of the Zhou Dynasty, according to which only the king had the right to make offers to Heaven on Mount Tai. Since Jisun was only a noble, he had no right to do so.

the contest ends, they drink and toast to each other. So they are quite like men of honor when they do contend."

3.8

Zixia asked about the connotation of a verse in the *Book of Songs*. "The pretty dimples of the artful smile, the well-defined black and white of the eyes, are like colorful patterns on plain silk."

The Master answered, "Only when you have a white base, can you paint colors on it."

Zixia said, "Can we then conclude that likewise, regulations and rituals come after humaneness?"

The Master said, "Zixia, you have thrown new light on this verse for me. I can now discuss the *Book of Songs* with you."

3.9

The Master said, "I can discourse on the rituals of the Xia Dynasty, but not on those of Qi (杞)[7] for lack of evidence. Similarly, I can discourse on the rituals of the state of Shang, but not on those of the state of Song[8]. The reason is there isn't much documentation on Qi and Song. If there were, I would be able to support what I say with evidence."

3.10

The Master said, "After the first offering of wine, I don't want to go on watching the Di ceremony."[9]

---

7. Its people said to be the descendants of Xia.
8. Its people said to be the descendants of Shang.
9. A ceremony for offering sacrifices to ancestors. Conducting the Di ceremonial service was reserved as the sole right of the King. Hence Confucius could not bear to see it conducted by the duke of the State of Lu.

3.11

Someone asked about the theory behind the Di ceremony. The Master answered, "I don't know." And pointing to his palm, he said, "He who knows what it is about may rule all under heaven as easily as placing something here."

3.12

When the Master offered sacrifices to the dead, he did so as if they were present. The same when he offered sacrifices to the gods. The Master said, "If I didn't do so, I might as well not offer any sacrifice ."

3.13

Wangsun Jia[10] asked about the saying "It is better to curry favor with the kitchen god than with Ao[11]."

The Master answered, "That is not so, because if you have offended Heaven, there is no one you can turn to in your prayer."

3.14

The Master said, "Zhou Dynasty established its own regulations and rituals by learning from the two previous dynasties[12]. And how rich its culture! That is why I am for Zhou."

3.15

When the Master entered the Grand Temple, he asked questions about everything there. Someone commented, "How can you say the son of that Zou official[13] knows the rituals well? When he entered the temple, he had to ask about everything."

On hearing this, the Master said, "It accords with the rituals to ask questions."

---

10. A minister of Wei.
11. A god believed to dwell in the southwest corner of a house.
12. Xia and Yin.
13. Referring to Confucius' father, Shuliang Ge.

3.16

The Master said, "In archery, the point is not to pierce the hide but to hit the target, for people differ in strength. That was a rule followed by the ancients."

3.17

Zigong wanted to do away with the offering of a live sheep during the sacrificial ceremony held on the first day of the Moon. The Master said, "Oh, Zigong! What you care for is the sheep, what I hold dear are the rituals."

3.18

The Master said, "In serving the ruler, one sticks to the rituals, but this is regarded as currying favor with him."

3.19

Duke Ding of Lu asked, "How should the ruler treat his ministers and how should the ministers serve their ruler?" Confucius answered, "The ruler should treat his ministers according to the rituals while the ministers should serve their ruler with devotion."

3.20

The Master said, "In *Guanju*[14], there is joy without wantonness, sadness without pain."

3.21

Duke Ai of Lu asked Zaiwo[15] what kind of timber to use when making a memorial tablet for the God of Earth. Zaiwo answered, "Xia used pinewood, Yin used cedar and Zhou used chestnut. It is said

---

14. The first poem in the *Book of Songs*.
15. Confucius' disciple.

that using the wood of the chestnut tree will cause the common people to tremble in awe.[16]

Hearing this, the Master commented, "One should not explain what has been done, nor should he try to advise against what is already accomplished. What's done is done."

3.22

The Master said, "Guan Zhong[17] had little capacity."

Someone asked, "Wasn't Guan Zhong frugal?"

The Master answered, "Guan Zhong had a large income from rents and a multitude of attendants. How could he be said to be frugal?"

"Didn't he know the rituals well?"

The Master answered, "The ruler of a state had screens; so did Guan Zhong. The former ruler had stands for emptied wine cups when he entertained other rulers; so did Guan Zhong. If you think Guan Zhong knew the rituals, then who doesn't?"

3.23

The Master discussed music with the Grand Music Master of Lu, saying, "This much can be said of it. When the piece begins, the different instruments all join in. Then, as it develops, it forms a harmonious melody with distinct rhythm, flowing on until it draws to an end."

3.24

An officer in the border region of Yi requested an audience with Confucius, saying, "I have never failed to meet with men of honor who have come my way." The disciples then presented him to the Master.

When he came out, he told them, "Don't you worry about him

---

16. Here Zaiwo is using a pun, because the "chestnut tree" and "tremble in awe" are homonyms in Chinese.
17. Chief minister of the State of Qi.

not having an official post. The world has long lost the Way. Heaven is about to use your master as a wooden bell to arouse the people."

3.25

The Master said of the music *Shao*[18], "It is the acme of perfection." Of the music *Wu*[19], he said, "It sounds beautiful enough, but not perfectly good."[20]

3.26

The Master said, "I cannot put up with a person who, while in high position, is lacking in tolerance, and who shows no reverence while performing the rituals and feels no grief while in mourning."

---

18. A piece of music passed down from the reign of the ancient king Shun.
19. A piece of music popular during the reign of King Wu of the Zhou Dynasty.
20. Shun inherited his reign peacefully from Yao, while King Wu seized the Ying Dynasty through war. To Confucius Shun was more virtuous.

Book 4

The passages in this book are pretty similar in form—many given as aphorisms—but different in content. They cover a variety of topics. A good many deal with the man of honor and his relationship with humaneness. Passages 4.18 to 4.21 again dwell on filial piety. Some well-known passages have become widely quoted mottos among the Chinese people, such as 4.5 (The man of honor will not seek wealth and rank by questionable means), 4.8 (If in the morning I have learnt the Way, I would have no regret dying the same evening.), 4.17 (When you meet a man of virtue, think of how you can become his equal; when you meet a man without virtue, examine yourself to see if you have the same faults.) and 4.25 (The man of honor is never alone. He is sure to enjoy the company of friends.).

4.1

The Master said, "It is beautiful to have your mind set on achieving humaneness. How can one say you are wise if you fail to do that?"

4.2

The Master said, "He who lacks humaneness can neither be content in poverty nor be happy for long in wealth. A man of honor rests at ease with humaneness, while a wise man chooses humaneness because it is advantageous for him to do so."

4.3

The Master said, "Only the humane knows how to love and how to hate."

4.4

The Master said, "He who sets his mind on achieving humaneness will be free from evil-doing."

4.5

The Master said, "Wealth and rank are what men desire, but the man of honor would not accept them unless they are obtained in a proper way. Poverty and lowliness are what men detest, but the man of honor would not try to get rid of them by means of an improper method. How can one be called a man of honor if he forsakes humaneness? Never for a moment should he do that. The man of honor clings to humaneness whether in moments of haste or in times of hardship."

4.6

The Master said, "I have yet to meet a man who truly loves humaneness, or a person who detests another because he lacks humaneness. He who detests those lacking in humaneness feels so because he does not want to be contaminated by what is inhumane. Is there anyone who can achieve humaneness through his efforts in a single day? I have never seen anyone who has that capacity. Perhaps there are, but I have yet to see one like that."

4.7

The Master said, "There are all types of people and all types of faults. Each one's faults can be traced to the type of people he belongs to.

By analyzing his faults, you will come to know the type of person he is."

4.8

The Master said, "If in the morning I have learned the Way, I would have no regret dying that same evening."

4.9

The Master said, "There is no point in soliciting the opinion of a scholar whose mind is set on learning the Way and yet is ashamed of his having to eat coarse grain and wear shabby clothes."

4.10

The Master said, "In dealing with the affairs of the state, there are no set rules as to what should be done or should not be done. Do what is reasonable and appropriate."

4.11

The Master said, "The man of honor cherishes virtue, the petty man cherishes his land. The man of honor is concerned about the sanctions of law, the petty man about the favors he hopes to receive."

4.12

The Master said, "He who allows himself to be motivated by self-interest will incur much ill-will."

4.13

The Master said, "What difficulty can one have if he governs the state by observing regulations and rituals and showing deference to others? If he cannot accomplish this, what use are the regulations and rituals to him?"

4.14

The Master said, "Do not worry about not having an official position. Worry about whether you are qualified for such a position. Do not worry when others don't appreciate your work. Rather, try to be worthy of being appreciated."

4.15

The Master said, "Cen, there is one thing that pervades my teachings."

Zeng Cen answered, "Yes, indeed."

After the Master had left, the other disciples asked Zeng Cen what Confucius was referring to.

Zeng Cen explained, "The Master simply meant that loyalty and forbearance form the essence of his teachings."

4.16

The Master said, "The man of honor thinks in terms of righteousness. The petty man in terms of gains."

4.17

The Master said, "When you meet a man of virtue, think how you can become his equal; when you meet a man without virtue, examine yourself to see if you are the same.

4.18

The Master said, "When serving your parents, be gentle when you try to dissuade them from doing wrong. Should your advice be ignored, remain reverent and obedient. Do not feel bitter even though laden with anxiety."

4.19

The Master said, "Do not travel to distant places when your parents are alive. If you have to do so, always let them know where you are."

4.20

The Master said, "You can be considered truly filial if you stick to your father's ways for three years after his death."

4.21

The Master said, "You must not ignore your parents' growing age, for it is something both to rejoice over and to be anxious about."

4.22

The Master said, "The ancients were sparing in words. They were afraid their deeds might not live up to their words."

4.23

The Master said, "Seldom does a man of restraint make mistakes."

4.24

The Master said, "The man of honor prefers to be slow in speech but quick in action."

4.25

The Master said, "The man of honor is never alone. He is sure to enjoy the company of friends."

4.26

Ziyou said, "Humiliation awaits those who insist on remonstrating with their rulers even when their advice has been rejected. Estrangement awaits those who insist on admonishing their friends even when their advice is not welcome."

Book 5

Confucius commented on many people in this book, both his disciples and famous statesmen in various states at the time, all on the issue of humaneness. He never minced his words, whether in praise or in condemnation. For instance, he noted that Zi Chan, a well known chief minister of the state of Zheng, had four virtues, in which he mentioned that besides being humble in his manners and respectful to his ruler, Zi Chan "was generous towards to the common people and just in using their services." In 5.26, a famous passage often quoted, Confucius, in comparing his pious wishes with those of his disciples Zilu and Yan Hui, said " I wish for the old to live in peace and comfort, for friends to trust each other, and for the young to be taken care of."

5.1
The Master said of Gongye Chang[1], "He would make a good husband. He was innocent though he was once imprisoned." He then had his daughter marry Gongye Chang.

---

1. Confucius' disciple.

5.2

The Master said of Nan Rong[2], "When the Way prevails in the country, he is not cast aside. When it no longer prevails, he stays away from punishment." He then had his niece marry Nan Rong.

5.3

When talking about Zijian[3], the Master said, "Here is a man of honor. If there were no men of honor in the State of Lu, where could he have acquired such virtue?"

5.4

Zigong asked, "What do you think of me?"

To which the Master answered, "You are like a vessel."

"What kind of a vessel?"

"Oh, a gemmed sacrificial vessel."[4]

5.5

Someone said, "Ran Yong is humane, but not eloquent."

The Master said, "What need is there for eloquence? He who is too clever in speech will be disliked by others. I cannot say whether Ran Yong is humane, but must he be eloquent?"

5.6

The Master wanted Qidiao Kai[5] to take an official post. But Qidiao Kai said, "I cannot trust myself to do so now." The Master was very pleased with the answer.

---

2. Confucius' disciple.
3. Confucius' disciple.
4. A vessel can only "serve one purpose", so here Confucius was implying that Zigong should work hard to become a man of honor who can serve different purposes, in short, an all-round person.
5. Confucius' disciple.

5.7

The Master said, "If the Way should fail to prevail, I would let myself drift on the sea aboard a raft and the only one to accompany me would be Zilu." On hearing this, Zilu was overjoyed. The Master then said, "Zilu's courage far surpasses mine, but he can't find the wood to build the raft."

5.8

Meng Wubo asked whether Zilu was humane. The Master said, "I cannot say he is." Meng repeated his question. The Master said, "Zilu can manage the military affairs of a state of one thousand chariots, but I don't know if he is humane."

Meng asked about Ranqiu.

The Master answered, "Ranqiu can be the magistrate of a town with one thousand households or the steward of a noble's manor with a hundred chariots, but I don't know if he is humane."

Meng then asked about Gongxi Hua[6].

The Master answered, "Gongxi Hua is suitable for conversing with guests when he wears his sash and takes his place at court, but I don't know if he is humane."

5.9

The Master asked Zigong, "Who is wiser? You or Yan Hui?"

Zigong answered, "How dare I compare myself with Yan Hui? When he is taught one thing, he understands ten. When I am taught one thing, I understand two."

The Master said, "Indeed, you and I are no match for Yan Hui."

5.10

Zai Yu (also known as Zaiwo) fell asleep during the day. The Master said, "One cannot carve on a piece of rotten wood, nor can one whitewash a wall of dried dung. What is the use of scolding a fellow

---

6. Confucius' disciple.

like him?" He added, "I used to listen to what people say and trust that they would act accordingly. Now I listen to what people say and observe how they act. Zai Yu has made me change my attitude."

5.11

The Master said, "I have never met anyone who is truly unyielding."

Someone suggested Sheng Cheng was such a person.

The Master said, "He is driven by desires, how can he be unyielding?"

5.12

Zigong said, "I don't want to do to others what I don't want them to do to me."

The Master commented, "Zigong, you have yet to live up to that saying."

5.13

Zigong said, "We have heard the Master talk about his views on ancient documents, but not about human nature and the Way of Heaven."

5.14

Zilu would not let himself be told anything new before he had put into practice what he had already learned.

5.15

Zigong asked, "Why was Kong Wenzi[7] called Wenzi[8]?"

The Master answered, "Because he was smart, eager to learn and was never ashamed to learn from those below his rank. That's why he was honored as Wenzi."

---

7. A minister of the State of Wei, named Kong Yue.
8. Posthumously named as Weizi, the cultured one.

5.16

When talking of Zi Chan[9], the Master said, "He had four virtues typical of a man of honor: he was humble in his manners, respectful to his ruler, generous towards the common people and just in using their services."

5.17

The Master said, "Yan Pingzhong[10] was good at making friends. The longer the friendship, the more he respected his friends."

5.18

The Master said, "Zang Wenzhong[11] kept a large tortoise in his house and for this pet, he had hills painted on the pillars and duckweeds on the raft posts. What is one to think of his intelligence?"[12]

5.19

Zizhang asked, "Zi Wen[13] gave no sign of pleasure on the three occasions when he was appointed Chief Minister, nor did he look unhappy on the three occasions when he was dismissed from that office. Moreover, before leaving his post, he always told his successors what had been done during his term of office. What do you think of him?"

The Master answered, "We can say that he was loyal."

Zizhang asked, "Can we say he was humane?"

The Master answered, "I don't know whether that can be called humaneness."

Zizhang asked again, "When Cui Zi[14] assassinated Duke Zhuang

---

9. A chief minister of the State of Zheng for whom Confucius had great respect.
10. A minister of Qi.
11. A minister of Lu.
12. The ancients in China worshipped the tortoise for its longevity, the bigger they were, the more precious. Here, Confucius was critical of Zang Wenzhong for, according to the rituals, only kings had the right to keep such tortoises.
13. The prime minister of Chu.
14. A minister of Qi.

(of Qi), Chen Wenzi[15] abandoned his ten carriages and left. After he arrived in another state, he said, 'The officials here are no better than Minister Cui Zi.' He left and went to yet another state. Again he said, 'The officials here are no better than Minister Cui Zi', whereupon he left again. What do you think of him?"

The Master said, "He was a man of integrity."

Zizhang asked, "But was he humane?"

The Master answered, "I don't know whether he is a humane person."

5.20

Ji Wenzi[16] always thought three times before taking action. When the Master heard about this, he commented, "Twice is enough."

5.21

The Master said, "Ning Wuzi[17] was intelligent when the Way prevailed in the country. He became 'stupid' when the Way no longer prevailed. Others could match him in intelligence, but no one could equal him in 'stupidity'."

5.22

When the Master was in the State of Chen, he said (to those who accompanied him), "Let's go home. Let's go home. My disciples at home are ambitious and already accomplished. Yet they don't know how to further refine themselves."

5.23

The Master said, "The brothers Bo Yi and Shu Qi bore no grudges against others for their past wrongs and that's why they incurred little ill will."

---

15. Another minister of Qi.
16. A minister of Lu.
17. A minister of Wei.

5.24

The Master said, "Who said Weisheng Gao was straight-forward? Once when someone wanted to borrow some vinegar from him, instead of saying that he didn't have any, he borrowed some from his neighbor and gave it to that man."

5.25

The Master said, "Flattery, hypocrisy and obsequiousness—these Zuo Qiuming[18] considered shameful. So do I. To hide one's hatred for someone and pretend friendliness—that Zuo Qiuming considered shameful. So do I."

5.26

Yan Hui and Zilu were with Confucius when he said, "Now tell me what you wish for most."

Zilu said, "I wish to share with my friends my carriages and horses, my clothes and furs, and never complain even if they spoil them."

Yan Hui said, "I wish never to boast of my merits or show off what I have done."

Zilu asked the Master, "What is your fondest wish?"

Confucius said, "I wish for the old to live in peace and comfort, for friends to trust each other, and for the young to be taken care of."

5.27

The Master said, "Alas! I have yet to find a man who is able to perceive his own errors and criticize himself for them."

5.28

The Master said, "In a small village of ten families, there are bound to be honest and trust-worthy people like me, but I don't think you will find anyone as eager to learn as I am."

---

18. A historian of Lu who was supposed to have written a history book named *Spring and Autumn*.

Book 6

The subject matter is again rather scattered. Many of the quotes concern Confucius' evaluation of his disciples. Some he praised; some he criticized or warned against possible mistakes; others he lamented their ill health. He used an interesting metaphor when he distinguished the humane person from the wise in 6.23 by saying that the wise loves the waters while the humane the mountains, the former loves activity while the latter tranquility.

In 6.18 Confucius dealt with the integration of substance and form, declaring that "substance without refinement is uncouth, but refinement with substance is pedantic". This is true both of man and the arts.

In 6.29, the Master announced that "the Mean embodies the highest form of virtue." By the Mean, he meant doing what is appropriate and not going to extremes. This is an important theme in Confucius' teaching and it has a profound influence on the Chinese psyche.

In 6.30, Confucius again characterized the humane, saying that he who helps others to establish what he himself wishes to establish and to achieve what he himself wishes to achieve is such a person. This is a positive way of pronouncing the Master's famous saying "Do not do unto others what you don't want others to do unto you."

6.9

When Minister Ji wanted to make Min Ziqian[6] the head of his Fei Estate, Min Ziqian begged the messenger to decline the offer for him. He said, "Should someone come again with the same offer, he would find me on the northern side of the Wen River[7]."

6.10

Boniu[8] became seriously ill. The Master paid him a call. Holding Boniu's hand, he said, "Alas, we are going to lose you. Such is fate. How sad that a man like you should contract such a disease! What a great misfortune!"

6.11

The Master said, "Yan Hui was truly virtuous. He had only a bamboo tube of grain to eat, a ladle of water to drink and a back alley to live in. Most people would find such a hard life intolerable. But Yan Hui did not allow it to affect his cheerfulness. How virtuous he was!"

6.12

Ranqiu said, "Not that I am unhappy with your teaching. It is just that I've run out of strength." The Master answered, "Those who have run out of their strength give up half way. You draw your limit even before starting."

6.13

The Master said to Zixia, "Be an honorable scholar, not a petty-minded pedant."

---

6. Confucius' disciple.
7. Implying he would flee to the State of Qi.
8. Confucius' disciple.

6.14

Ziyou became the county head of Wu. The Master asked him, "Have you found any talented people there?"

Ziyou answered, "There is one named Tantai Mieming[9]. He never takes shortcuts and he never calls on me at my house except on official business."

6.15

The Master said, "Meng Zhifan[10] was never given to boasting about himself. Once, when his army was retreating, he stayed in the rear to cover his forces. But as they approached their own city gate, he goaded his horse on, shouting, 'I stayed at the rear not out of courage, it is just that my horse wouldn't go any faster.'"

6.16

The Master said, "In today's world, it would be difficult for you to escape trouble if you had only the good looks of Song Chao[11] but not the eloquence of Zhu Tuo[12]."

6.17

The Master said, "Who can get out of a house but by a door? How is it then that no one is following the Way?"

6.18

The Master said, "Substance without refinement is uncouth. But refinement without substance is pedantic. Only when substance and refinement are well blended can there be a man of honor."

---

9. Later to become Confucius' disciple.
10. A minister of Lu.
11. A prince of the State of Song who had twice caused great disturbance in his country because of his good looks and illicit affairs with Nan Zi.
12. A minister of Wei.

6.19

The Master said, "Man is born to be upright. He who is not upright survives by mere chance."

6.20

The Master said, "To enjoy knowledge is better than to acquire knowledge. To love knowledge is better than both."

6.21

The Master said, "You can discuss profundity only with those above average, but not with those below average."

6.22

Fan Chi asked about wisdom. The Master said, "Give to the common people what is their due, respect the ghosts and spirits but keep a distance from them – that is wisdom."

Fan Chi asked about humaneness. The Master said, "The humane thinks first of overcoming the difficulties and then of enjoying the benefits. That is humaneness indeed."

6.23

The Master said, "The wise love the waters, the humane love the mountains. The wise love activity, the humane tranquility. The wise enjoy life, the humane are blessed with longevity."

6.24

The Master said, "With reform, the State of Qi can equal Lu; with reform, Lu can attain the Way."[13]

---

13. Lu, whose first duke being the son of Duke Zhou, was considered by Confucius as the model of Duke Zhou's tradition.

6.25

The Master sighed, "A cornered vessel[14] without corners! What cornered vessel is this!"[15]

6.26

Zaiwo asked, "If a man of honor were told that another of his kind had fallen into a well, would he jump in to save the latter?"

The Master answered, "Why should that be? A man of honor will try to rescue the man in the well, but he won't jump in himself. He may be deceived, but he will not act foolishly."

6.27

The Master said, "A man of honor will not go astray, for he is widely read and cultured and he keeps himself in line with the rituals."

6.28

The Master called on Nan Zi[16]. Zilu was unhappy about the visit. The Master swore, "If I have done anything improper, may Heaven reject me! May Heaven reject me!"[17]

6.29

The Master said, "The Mean(中庸 *zhongyong*) embodies the highest form of virtue. Yet it has long been found lacking among the common people."

---

14. It's used for drinking.
15. In ancient times, the sacrificial wine vessel named Gu used to be four-cornered. By Confucius' time, it had become round-bottomed. Here, Confucius was complaining about those who had cast away tradition.
16. The consort of Duke Ling of Wei.
17. Nan Zi had a bad reputation because she was said to be lascivious and had undue influence in the Wei court.

6.30

Zigong asked the Master, "What do you think of someone who gives extensively to the common people and provides aid to the multitude? Would you say he is humane?"

The Master answered, "He is far more than being humane. He must be a sage. Even Yao and Shun could not have done as much. A humane person is one who helps others establish what he himself wishes to establish and to achieve what he himself wishes to achieve. To be able to correlate one's own feelings with those of others may be the best way to approach humaneness."

Book 7

Here in this book Confucius described himself as one, studying hard and teaching others tirelessly (7.2), two, being used to plain living so that to him riches are nothing more than sailing clouds (7.16) and three, being so immersed in his studies that he forgets his meals, so happy that he forgets his worries and does not know the approach of old age (7.16). Another famous passage is about retaining a humble attitude so that you can always learn from the people around you(7.22). "Walking in the company of others there is bound to be something I can learn from them. Their good traits I follow; their bad ones I try to avoid." Environmentalists today might be pleasingly surprised to learn that the Master was a true lover of Nature, that when he fished he never used a net to haul a big catch and when he hunted he never touched a roosting bird (7.27).

7.1
The Master said, "I transmit but do not create. I'm a believer in and an admirer of the ancients. In my mind, I compare myself to Lao Peng[1].

---

1. Commentators differ as to whether "Lao Peng" refers to one person or two persons.

7.2

The Master said, "To remember what I have learned, to study hard and never feel contented, to teach others tirelessly, which of these goals are beyond me?"

7.3

The Master said, "Failure to cultivate virtue and review what I have learned, inability to practice what I have been told to be righteous and unwillingness to correct my mistakes—these are what worries me."

7.4

During his moments of leisure at home, the Master appeared relaxed and cheerful.

7.5

The Master said, "How I have aged! It has been a long time since I dreamed of the Duke of Zhou[2]."

7.6

The Master said, "I set my mind on the Way, persist in virtue, rely upon humaneness and delight in the arts."

7.7

The Master said, "I have never refused to teach any disciple who offered me ten strips of dried meat[3]."

---

2. The Duke of Zhou was the brother of King Wu. Tradition had it that he established the rituals and regulations of the time. He was therefore greatly admired by Confucius.
3. Ten strips of dried meat was a common gift in ancient China presented on one's first visit to a teacher's home.

7.8

The Master said, "I do not try to enlighten my disciples until they have tried hard but failed to understand something. I do not supply my disciples with any new vocabulary or put their ideas into words for them unless they have difficulty doing so. When I have given them one instance and they cannot draw inferences from it, I do not repeat my lesson."

7.9

The Master would never eat his fill by the side of a mourner.

7.10

If Confucius had wept at a funeral, he would not sing for the rest of the day.

7.11

The Master said to Yan Hui, "Only you and I are able to advance when called upon but prefer to stay in the background when neglected."

Zilu asked, "If you were to lead a grand army, whom would you like to take along with you?"

The Master answered, "I would not take along with me someone who would wrestle with a tiger with bare hands, or try to ford a river and die without regret. Instead, I would want someone who was thoughtful, cautious and capable of realizing his goal by strategy."

7.12

The Master said, "If wealth were an acceptable goal, then I wouldn't mind being a whip-holding guard for the marketplace. If it weren't, I'd rather follow my own inclination."[4]

---

4. Being a whip-holding guard for the marketplace was considered a lowly job in ancient China.

7.13

The Master was cautious when dealing with three matters: fasting before offering sacrifice, war and illness.

7.14

The Master heard the *Shao*[5] when he was in the State of Qi. For several months he did not notice what the meat he ate tasted like. He said, "I had no idea that music could be so wonderful!"

7.15

Ranyou wanted to know if the Master supported the ruler of Wei. Zigong said, "Alright, I shall go and find out."

He went in and asked, "What sort of people were Bo Yi and Shu Qi?"

The Master answered, "Men of virtue in ancient times."

Zigong asked, "Did they have any regret?"

"They sought to be humane and they attained their goal. Why should they have any regret?"

On coming out, Zigong said, "The Master does not support the ruler of Wei."[6]

7.16

The Master said, "There is joy in eating coarse grain, drinking plain water and using my elbow for a pillow. To me, riches and honors attained immorally are mere drifting clouds."

7.17

The Master said, "Let me live a few more years so that I may, at fifty,

---

5. Ancient music of Shun.
6. Confucius did not support the ruler of Wei because he fought against his own father for the throne, whereas the brothers Bo Yi and Shu Qi both declined to ascend the throne.

study the *Book of Changes*. Then I shall manage to avoid making serious mistakes."

7.18

The Master sometimes used the Yayan when reciting the *Book of Songs* and the *Book of Records* or performing the rituals.[7]

7.19

When the lord of She asked Zilu about Confucius, Zilu failed to give him an answer. Later the Master said to Zilu, "Why didn't you say something like this: He is the sort of person who is so immersed in his studies that he forgets his meals, who is so happy that he forgets his worries, and who knows not the approach of old age."

7.20

The Master said, "I was not born with knowledge, but being an admirer of antiquity, I was eager to acquire knowledge about it."

7.21

The Master never discussed miracles, the use of force, disorders and spirits.

7.22

The Master said, "Walking in the company of others, there is bound to be something I can learn from them. Their good traits I follow; their bad ones I try to avoid."

---

7. As the language used in the capital of Zhou, Yayan was the lingua franca of the Zhou Dynasty. Yayan was different from the various dialects used in Lu and other states. Ordinarily, Confucius spoke in the dialect of Lu.

7.23

The Master said, "Heaven bestowed virtue on me, what can Huan Tui do to me?"[8]

7.24

The Master said, "You, my pupils, do you think that I have kept something from you? No, there is nothing that I do which I don't share with you. That's me."

7.25

The Master taught four disciplines: historical documents, social conduct, loyalty to superiors and faithfulness to friends.

7.26

The Master said, "I cannot hope to meet a sage. Meeting a man of honor would give me satisfaction."

He added, "I cannot hope to meet a good man. Meeting a man who sticks to his principles would give me satisfaction. A man can hardly stick to his principles if he pretends to be full when he's empty and to be at ease when he is in difficult circumstance."

7.27

The Master fished with a line but never with a net. He used corded arrows to shoot birds but never a roosting one.

7.28

The Master said, "There are those who can do without knowledge, but I am not one of them. I listen to many views and choose the sound ones to follow. I see many things and keep them in my memory. Knowledge attained this way is the second best."[9]

---

8. Huan Tui was a general of Song who attempted to kill Confucius.
9. According to Confucius, innate knowledge is superior to his type of knowledge.

7.29

People of Huxian were difficult to communicate with.[10] When a boy from that region came and was received by Confucius, his disciples were puzzled. The Master said, "What I approve of is his progress, not his backwardness. Why be so exacting? When a person makes an effort to become a better person, I welcome his progress although I cannot vouch for his past."

7.30

The Master said, "Is humaneness really so remote? I've only to wish for it and it will come to me."

7.31

The Minister of Justice asked whether Duke Zhao of Lu knew the rituals. Confucius answered, "Yes, he does."

After Confucius had left, Chen approached Wuma Qi[11] and greeted him, saying, "It is said that a man of honor is never partial, but it seems to me that some men of honor are. The Duke took a lady from the State of Wu as his wife even though she had the same clan name as his and renamed her Wu Mengzi. If the Duke knew the rituals, who doesn't?"

When Wuma Qi passed on this comment to Confucius, the Master said, "How fortunate I am! Whenever I make a mistake, others are sure to notice it."

7.32

When the Master sang along with other people and found a good singer among them, he would always have the song sung again and then join in.

---

10. Because they spoke a strange dialect.
11. Confucius' disciple.

7.33

The Master said, "In classics, I'm no worse than anyone else, but I have yet to become a man of honor who practices what he has learned."

7.34

The Master said, "How would I dare to consider myself a sage or a man of honor? Perhaps it can be said I tried unflaggingly to become one and to teach without growing weary, that is all." Gongxi Hua said, "That is precisely what we disciples have not been able to emulate."

7.35

The Master was seriously ill. Zilu asked for permission to pray for him. The Master asked, "Was this ever done before?"

Zilu answered, "Yes. The 'Prayer' says, 'we pray for you to the gods above and below.'"

The Master said, "In that case, I've been saying my prayers all along[12]."

7.36

The Master said, "Extravagance leads to arrogance, and frugality to shabbiness. I would rather be shabby than arrogant."

7.37

The Master said, "The man of honor has peace of mind, while the petty-minded man is constantly troubled by anxiety."

7.38

The Master was stern but cordial, awe-inspiring but not overbearing, dignified but easy to approach.

---

12. A polite way of expressing displeasure.

Book 8

Passage 8.9 is one of the most contentious of Confucius' sayings. It states, "One can make the common people follow a course of action but must not let them understand why they should do so." Such an attitude towards the people was typical of feudal government. Nowadays, in a civil society the people have the right of being informed, and speedily so in our internet age.

There is also in this book a famous quote (8.7) from Confucius' disciple, Master Zeng, which states a scholar must be strong and steadfast since it is his lifelong task to practice humaneness.

8.1

The Master said, "Tai Bo can be said to be a man of the highest virtue. Several times he gave up his claim to the throne (in favor of his younger brother Ji Li). The common people could not find an adequate expression to praise him."

8.2

The Master said, "Without observing the rituals, courtesy would become tiresome labor, caution would turn to cowardice, courage would lead to disturbance, and straight-forwardness to acrimony. When the ruler devotes himself to his parents, the common people will aspire to humaneness. When he does not forsake his friends, his people will not treat each other meanly."

8.3

Master Zeng was ill. He summoned his disciples and said to them, "Look at my feet and look at my hands. The *Book of Songs* says, 'trembling and shaking as if approaching a deep abyss, as if walking on thin ice.'[1] I know I am spared of trouble. Take care, young friends!"

8.4

When Master Zeng was ill, Meng Jing Zi[2] visited him. Master Zeng said, "When a bird is about to die, its cries are mournful. When a man is about to die, his words are well-intended. There are three principles of conduct a man of honor values most. In appearance, be composed and thus avoid wantonness and tardiness; in demeanor, cling to good faith and thus invite trust; in speech, be careful with words and thus avoid vulgarity and impropriety. As to the details of liturgy, leave them to the minor officials who are in charge."

8.5

Master Zeng said, "I had a friend who pursued this rule of conduct: to be capable and yet ask for advice from the less capable; to be knowledgeable and yet consult the less knowledgeable; to have and yet seem to lack; to be full and yet seem to be empty; to be offended and yet not to mind."

8.6

Master Zeng said, "If a person can be entrusted with an orphaned young ruler and the destiny of a state of a hundred square *li*[3], if he

---

1. This quote from the *Book of Songs* was aimed at showing that one's body belonged to his parents and must be preserved as a sign of filial piety.
2. A minister of Lu.
3. One *li* equals 0.5 kilometer, or 0.311 mile.

can be unyielding in moments of crisis, then he is indeed a man of honor."

8.7

Master Zeng said, "A scholar must be strong and steadfast, for his burden is heavy and his journey long. Since his task is to practice humaneness, is the burden not heavy? Since till death does his journey end, is it not long?"

8.8

The Master said, "In the *Book of Songs*, one finds inspiration; in rituals, the way to establishment; in music, self-perfection."

8.9

The Master said, "One can make the common people follow a course of action, but must not let them understand why they should do so."

8.10

The Master said, "Those who are brave but cannot tolerate poverty are likely to cause trouble. So are those who lack virtue and are despised."

8.11

The Master said, "Should a man as gifted as the Duke of Zhou be arrogant and niggardly, then his other qualities are not worth looking at."

8.12

The Master said, "It is hard to find one who has studied for three years without thinking about his career."

8.13

The Master said, "Stick to the love of learning and abide by the Way till death. Do not enter a state which is unstable and do not live in a state which is in turmoil. Be visible when the Way prevails. Be invisible when it does not. It is shameful to be poor and humble when the Way prevails. It is equally shameful to be prosperous and in high position when the Way does not prevail."

8.14

The Master said, "While not in office, do not discuss official policies."

8.15

The Master said, "When master musician Zhi of Lu began to play *The Cry of the Osrey*, the music reached a crescendo, and what a flood of wonderful notes filled the ears."

8.16

The Master said, "Men who are ambitious but are not upright, men who are ignorant yet inattentive, men who are incapable and untrustworthy—these are people I cannot appreciate."

8.17

The Master said, "Study as if you might not reach your objective and as if you might forget what you have learned."

8.18

The Master said, "How lofty Shun and Yu were! All under Heaven was theirs and yet this meant nothing to them."

8.19

Confucius said, "What a great sovereign Yao[4] was! Nothing is greater than Heaven. Yao alone took it upon himself to make Heaven his model. So great were his blessings that the people could find no word to praise him. How splendid his achievements! How brilliant his cultural accomplishments!"

8.20

Shun had five ministers and all under Heaven was well governed. King Wu of Zhou said, "I have ten capable ministers."

Confucius commented, "Isn't it true that talents are really hard to find? After Yao and Shun, King Wu possessed the greatest number of talented people, but one of his ministers was a woman[5], so actually he had nine. King Wen[6] had two-thirds of the empire, yet (because of his loyalty, he did not overthrow the Yin Dynasty) he continued to pay homage to Yin. The virtue displayed by the house of Zhou can be said to have reached the zenith."

8.21

The Master said, "With Yu I can find no fault. He ate simple food but offered grand sacrifices to the ancestral spirits. He wore coarse clothes but dressed magnificently on sacrificial occasions. He lived in a humble house but devoted his all to fighting the floods. With Yu I can find no fault."

---

4. Besides Shun and Yu, Yao was another ruler whom Confucius considered to be a sage.
5. King Wu's mother.
6. The father of King Wu.

Book 9

There are two famous quotes in this book. Stressing the strength of the individual will, Confucius states in 9.26, "You can deprive an army of its commanding officer, but you cannot deprive a man of his aspirations."

In 9.28, he states "only in the cold of winter is the point brought home that pines and cypresses are the last to fade," meaning hard times are the best test of a man's character. In 9.8, Confucius says. "Am I a learned man? No, I am not. If a farmer asks me a question, my mind is a total blank...." Compare this with Socrates' statement, "I know that I don't know."

9.1

Seldom did the Master touch on the subject of personal gain. Not so, on the subjects of fate and humaneness.

9.2

A man from Daxiang village said, "Confucius is great indeed. He is learned, yet he has made no effort to make himself famous." When the Master heard this, he said to his disciples, "What shall I take up for my occupation? Chariot-driving or archery? I think I prefer chariot-driving."

9.3

The Master said, "A hemp cap is what is prescribed by the rituals (when one steps into an ancestral temple). But now, a silk one is used instead. I follow the former practice since it is more economical. To kowtow before ascending the steps (when a minister is received by the sovereign who is seated on a podium) is what is required by the rituals. But now, one kowtows only after having ascended the steps. This is being disrespectful. So, although it is against common practice today, I stick to the old way."

9.4

The Master was free of four defects. He never made groundless speculation, did not claim absolute certainty, was not inflexible, and was not self-centered.

9.5

Trapped in Kuang, the Master said, "After King Wen passed away, has not Zhou's culture been vested in me? If Heaven had intended to destroy it, we latecomers would not have been vested with it. Since Heaven did not intend to have it destroyed, how can the men of Kuang do any harm to me?"

9.6

The Grand Minister asked Zigong, "Is your master a sage? If he is, why is he skilled in so many ways?" Zigong answered, "Precisely because Heaven has made him a sage, he is capable of many skills."

On hearing this, the Master said, "Does the Grand Minister know me? I am of humble origin. That's why I excel in so many menial skills. Would somebody with an aristocratic background need to master such skills? No, he needn't."

9.7

Lao quoted the Master as saying, "Because I have not taken up any official post, I have to learn so many different arts."

9.8

The Master said, "Am I a learned man? No, I am not. But if a farmer asks me a question and my mind is a total blank, I shall keep turning the question over in my mind and weighing its various aspects until I come up with an answer."

9.9

The Master said, "The Phoenix does not appear. The River presents no chart. Alas! I am done for."[1]

9.10

When the Master saw people in mourning clothes or ceremonial robes, or when he saw a blind person, even if they were younger in age, he would rise. When walking past them, he would quicken his steps to show respect.

9.11

Yan Hui said with a sigh, "The more I look up to the Master's teachings, the more lofty they seem to be. The more I delve into them, the more profound they become. I see them before me, suddenly they are behind me. The Master is adept at leading me on step by step. He has broadened my mind with knowledge and restrained me with the rituals. I could not give up my studies even if I wanted to. Having exerted myself to the best of my ability, I seem to have made some achievement, but to go further, I am still at a loss."

---

1. Legend had it that when the phoenix appeared and a chart be afloat on the river, a golden age would come.

9.12

The Master was seriously ill. Zilu asked his fellow disciples to act as retainers in mourning as for a lord. When his condition improved, the Master said, "Zilu, this farce has lasted too long. I am not entitled to have these retainers. Whom are we trying to fool? Heaven? Besides, I would rather have you, my disciples, and not the retainers at my bedside when I die. I may not be given an elaborate funeral, but I would not be left to die by the wayside, would I?"[2]

9.13

Zigong asked, "Suppose you had a piece of beautiful jade, would you put it away in a safe, or would you sell it to one who knows its worth?" The Master said, "I would sell it! Yes, sell it! I'm just waiting for the right buyer."[3]

9.14

The Master wanted to move and settle among the Nine Tribes of the East. Someone told him, "The place is pretty wild. How would you be able to cope?" The Master answered, "Can you still consider it wild once a man of honor settles down there?"

9.15

The Master said, "It was only after my return from Wei to Lu that the music was put in the right order and the *Ya* and the *Song*[4] were restored to their proper places."

---

2. During Confucius' time, only ministers kept retainers in their house. Confucius, having retired from his official post, had no retainers. He, therefore, disapproved of Zilu's arrangement which he considered presumptuous.
3. Confucius and Zigong were using beautiful jade as a metaphor for talented people. This passage shows how eager Confucius was for an official post to carry out his political program.
4. Sections of the *Book of Songs*, which could be translated as odes and hymns

9.16

The Master said, "Serve the high officials in public life, tend to the elders at home, spare no effort in funeral arrangements and not be overcome by drinking—which of these are beyond my ability?"

9.17

Standing by a river, the Master declared, "Thus time flows by, never ceasing day or night."

9.18

The Master said, "I have yet to meet a man who loves virtue as much as beauty."

9.19

The Master said, "It's like building a mound. If I stopped before the last basket of earth, I would never complete the job. It's like filling a hollow. Even if I have tipped in only the first basketful of earth, it would be a step forward if I kept at it."

9.20

The Master said, "If there's anyone who can listen to me with unflagging attention, it has to be Yan Hui."

9.21

Speaking of Yan Hui, the Master said, "Alas, he is gone. I saw him always making progress, never stopping in his effort."

9.22

The Master said, "There are saplings that fail to blossom and saplings that blossom but fail to bear fruit."

9.23

The Master said, "The young should be regarded with awe. How do we know the next generation will not surpass the present? However, those who have reached the age of forty or fifty, yet still haven't achieved anything to distinguish themselves, need not be taken seriously."

9.24

The Master said, "How can one not heed the serious and earnest words of criticism uttered by others? What is important is that he corrects himself. How can one not be pleased when he hears agreeable words? What is important is that he analyzes what has been said. I can do nothing with those who are pleased with what others say, but do not analyze, or who agree with everything being said, but do not correct themselves."

9.25

The Master said, "Make it your primary principle to be faithful and trustworthy. Do not accept as friends those whose moral quality is inferior to your own. When you make a mistake, do not be afraid to correct it."

9.26

The Master said, "You can deprive an army of its commanding officer, but you cannot deprive a man of his aspirations."

9.27

The Master said, "If there is anyone wearing a worn-out gown standing beside a man dressed in fur and not feeling ashamed, I suppose it must be Zilu. 'Neither envious nor covetous, how can he be anything but good.'[5]" On hearing himself praised, Zilu then frequently

---

5. A quote from the *Book of Songs*.

chanted those lines, whereupon the Master said, "Is that quality alone enough?"

9.28

The Master said, "Only in the cold of winter is the point brought home that pines and cypresses are the last to fade."

9.29

The Master said, "The wise are not perplexed, the humane do not worry and the brave have no fear."

9.30

The Master said, "A companion in study may not be a companion in the pursuit of the Way. A companion in the pursuit of the Way may not share your stand. And he who shares your stand may not share your moral discretion."

9.31

"The flowers of the *tangti* tree,
    How gracefully they dance.
    Not that I do not miss you,
    It's just that your home is so far away."[6]
    The Master commented, "The poet did not really miss her. If he did, her being far away would not have been a problem."

---

6. A poem from the *Book of Songs*.

Book 10

This book is unique both in content and style. There is no dialogue. With two exceptions, the passages do not mention Confucius. We could take it for granted that they refer to the Master. Nearly all of them concern decorum, both in the presence of other officials attending court and at home. These range from manners to dresses and body languages, and even including eating and sleeping habits. When we compare the etiquette of Confucius' time with that of ours today, we become aware how liberated we are now! This does not mean we can do away with manners, which is necessary in any society where there exist inter-personal relationships.

10.1

In his own village, Confucius appeared very respectful, as if at a loss for words. In the ancestral temple or at court, he spoke articulately but was selective of words.

10.2

At court, when conversing with junior ministers, he spoke freely and affably; when conversing with senior ministers, he spoke respectfully.

In the presence of the ruler, he showed reverence and uneasiness, and his steps became gentle.

10.3

Summoned by the ruler to receive foreign guests, he looked solemn, and his legs moved briskly. He greeted those lined up on both sides with his hands clasped, now to the left and now to the right; and his robes followed his movements without being disarranged. When he went forward (to greet the guests) with quickened steps, it seemed he was gliding on wings. When the guests had left, he invariably reported back to his ruler, "The guests are out of sight."

10.4

On entering the gate of the duke's court, Confucius appeared uneasy and cautious as though there was little room for him there.

He dared not stand in the doorway, or tread on the threshold.

As he walked past where the ministers stood, he wore a solemn look and quickened his steps, speaking only in a soft tone.

When the audience began, he lifted the hem of his robe respectfully (as he ascended the steps) and it seemed he could hardly breathe.

Only when the audience had ended and he began to descend the steps did he breathe a sigh of relief and relax.

When he got to the bottom of the steps, he picked up speed as if on wings.

Once back in his place, he resumed his humble countenance.

10.5

(At the ceremony to meet a foreign mission, he bent his body slightly forward,) the jade tablet[1] seemed too heavy for him to carry. When he raised it with both hands, he seemed to be greeting; when he lowered it, he seemed ready to hand it to someone else. His solemn look

---

1. A symbol of authority given to him by his ruler.

gave the impression he was engaged in serious business. He walked with short steps along a single line.

When presenting the gifts, he looked amiable and courteous.

When meeting in a private capacity with the hosts, he appeared relaxed and cheerful.

10.6

The man of honor does not use reddish black or dark grey for borders, nor red or violet for casual clothes.

In the heat of summer, he wears an unlined gown made of hemp or linen, making sure it covers the undergarment.

(In winter,) he wears a black gown over a black lambskin, a white gown over a fawnskin robe and a yellow gown over yellow fox fur.

His informal fur coat is long but with a short right sleeve.

He requires his quilt to be one and half times his height.

Fox and raccoon pelts are used for cushions because their fur is thick.

He places no restrictions on the kind of ornament he wears once a period of mourning is over.

For non-ceremonial occasions, his gowns are made shorter.

Lambskin coats and black caps are not to be worn at funerals.

On the first day of the New Year, he invariably goes to the palace in full court attire.

10.7

In period of fasting, he invariably wears a cotton bathrobe. He also changes to a more simple diet and to another seat.

10.8

(To Confucius) rice could never be over-husked and meat could never be too finely cut.

He did not eat staple food which had gone bad or fish and meat which had spoiled. He did not eat food whose color had changed or which had a bad smell. He did not touch food which was not properly prepared or when it was not the season for eating it. He did not eat meat which had not been slaughtered properly, or served without the proper sauce.

Even when there was plenty of meat, he avoided eating more meat than grain.

Only in drinking, he did not set himself a limit, but he never allowed himself to become drunk.

He did not touch wine or dried meat bought from the market. Ginger he took at the end of each meal, but not in great amount.

10.9

When assisting at a sacrificial ceremony with the ruler, he would not keep his portion of the sacrificial meat overnight. In other cases, he would not keep the sacrificial meat for more than three days. Beyond three days, he would not touch it.[2]

10.10

He would not converse during meals, nor would he talk before retiring for the night.

10.11

Even if his meal consisted of only coarse grain and vegetable soup, he would offer a sacrifice at each meal, with the same solemnity as during fasting.

10.12

He would not sit unless the mat was set properly.

---

2. In ancient times, the ministers accompanied the ruler at sacrificial ceremonies, after which they would be granted a piece of sacrificial meat. As the ceremonies usually lasted two days, it would be at least more than three days if and when they ate the meat.

10.13

When drinking at a village gathering, he would not leave until those with walking sticks[3] had done so.

10.14

When an exorcism was performed in his village, he would attend in his court robe standing on the steps facing east (where the host usually stood to welcome his guests).

10.15

When asking someone to extend his respects to a friend in another state, he would bow deeply twice, before sending him off.[4]

10.16

When presented with some medicine by Ji Kangzi, the Master accepted it with a deep bow. However, he said, "Not knowing its effects, I dare not try it."

10.17

The stable caught fire. Hurrying back from the court, the Master asked, "Was anyone hurt?" He did not ask about the horses.

10.18

When the ruler granted him some cooked food, he would set his mat straight and taste the food immediately. When granted uncooked meat, he would first cook it and offer it to his ancestors. When granted a live animal, he would rear it. When accompanying the ruler at a meal, he would eat only the rice while the ruler performed the sacrificial offering.

---

3. Referring to the elderly.
4. One of the bows being meant for his friend.

10.19

When he was ill and the ruler went to see him, Confucius made sure to lie with his head to the east[5] with his court robe draped over him (to show his respect), the sash dangling.

10.20

When the ruler summoned him, he would set off on foot without waiting for his carriage to be yoked.

10.21

When he went inside the Grand Temple, he inquired about everything.

10.22

When a friend died and there was no kin to take care of his funeral service, the Master would say, "Leave it to me."

10.23

He would not bow when accepting gifts from a friend, even if they were carriages and horses, the only exception being sacrificial meat.

10.24

When he slept, he did not lie flat on his back like a corpse. When alone at home, he did not sit as he would receiving a guest.

10.25

When he saw someone in mourning, whether he was a close friend or not, he would change his expression to show sympathy. When he

---

5. The direction from which the ruler would enter.

saw someone wearing a ceremonial cap or someone blind, even if it were a casual meeting, he would show respect.

On passing someone carrying costume for the dead, he would lean forward with his hands on the cross bar by way of showing respect. He would act in a similar manner toward someone carrying official documents.

When a sumptuous feast was brought in, his face would assume a solemn expression and he would rise to his feet.

His countenance would change with a clap of thunder or a strong gust of wind.

10.26

When mounting a carriage, he would first stand upright and hold on to the hand rail to pull himself up.

Once in his seat, he would not look inside the carriage, nor talk volubly, nor point his fingers around.

10.27

(Confucius and Zilu came upon some pheasants.) The Master's face lit up. Startled, the birds took flight. They circled for a while before alighting. Confucius exclaimed, "Pheasants on the mountain ridge! It is the season! It is the season!" Zilu cupped one hand in the other (in a symbol of respect), but the pheasants flapped their wings three times and flew away.[6]

---

6. Since ancient times, scholars have not been able to find a satisfactory explanation for the significance of this passage.

Book 11

Confucius' comments in this book were nearly all about his disciples. In one passage (11.21), he spoke without referring to any of them. "I applaud someone who speaks sincerely," he said, "However, we need to find out whether he is really a man of honor, or he is simply appearing to be sincere." Passage 11.26 is a long one. It shows the Master asking four of his disciples what they would do if given the chance to show their talent. The different answers are indicative of their unique characters and inclinations, and the Master's response is intriguing.

11.1

The Master said, "Those who first studied the rituals and music with me were usually rustics. Those who later studied them with me were usually from the aristocracy. If I could choose between them, I would prefer the former."

11.2

The Master said, "None of those who were with me in Chen and Cai are here with me now."[1]

1. Yan Hui, Zilu and Zigong had accompanied Confucius when he visited the States of Chen and Cai where they suffered hunger and other hardships. Now,

11.3

(The disciples each had his own outstanding points.) Virtuous in conduct, there were Yan Hui, Min Ziqian, Ran Boniu and Zhong Gong. Eloquent in speech, there were Zai Wo and Zigong. Capable in governance, there were Ranyou and Zilu. Knowledgeable in culture, there were Ziyou and Zixia.

11.4

The Master said, "Yan Hui is of no help to me. He is pleased with everything I say."

11.5

The Master said, "Min Ziqian is filial indeed. No one disagrees with his parents and brothers when they praised him."[2]

11.6

Nan Rong read the verse about the white jade scepter over and over. Confucius therefore married his niece to him.[3]

11.7

Ji Kangzi asked Confucius which of his disciples were eager to learn. The Master answered, "There was Yan Hui who was eager to learn. Unfortunately he died young. Now there is none."

11.8

When Yan Hui died, (his father) Yan Lu asked the Master to sell his carriage in order to pay for an outer coffin for his son. The Master said, "Everyone speaks for his son, whether he is talented or not.

---

2. Yan Hui and Zilu had died and Zigong had left Confucius. The Master was thus expressing his sorrow at the loss of the former two.
3. The verse in the *Book of Songs* says: One can erase a black spot on a white jade scepter, but not the flaws in one's speech.

When my son Li died, he had a coffin but no outer coffin. I could not go around on foot just in order to provide him with an outer coffin because it would be improper for me, a former official, to travel on foot."

11.9

When Yan Hui died, the Master said, "Alas! Heaven has destroyed me. Heaven has destroyed me."

11.10

When Yan Hui died, the Master wept bitterly. His disciples said, "Master, you are over-grieved." The Master said, "Am I? If I do not grieve for him, who else should I grieve for?"

11.11

When Yan Hui died, the disciples wanted to hold a grand funeral for him. The Master said, "You mustn't do that." All the same, the disciples went ahead and buried him in grand style. The Master said, "Hui, you treated me like I were your father, but I have not been able to treat you like a son. This is not my fault, but that of your fellow disciples."

11.12

Zilu asked about serving the ghosts and spirits. The Master said, "Why should one worry about serving the ghosts and spirits when he is not even able to serve the living?"

Zilu went on, "May I ask about death?"

The Master said, "How can one understand death when he doesn't even understand life?"

11.13

Standing in attendance on the Master, Min Ziqian looked respectful and honest, Zilu looked firm and staunch, Ranyou and Zigong gentle and affable. The Master was pleased, but he commented, "A man like Zilu will probably not die a natural death[4]."

11.14

The Chief Minister of Lu wanted to rebuild the treasury. Min Ziqian said, "Can it not be renovated? Why must it be rebuilt?"

The Master said, "Here is a man of few words. Yet when he speaks, he hits the nail on the head."

11.15

The Master said, "What is Zilu doing, playing the Se[5] in my house?" From then on, the other disciples ceased to treat Zilu with respect. The Master then said, "Zilu may have entered the main hall, but not the inner chamber."[6]

11.16

Zigong asked, "Who is the better of the two, Zizhang or Zixia?" The Master said, "Zizhang tends to go too far. With Zixia, it is not far enough."

"Does that make Zizhang better?"

"Going too far is just as bad as not going far enough."

---

4. Meaning he is too quick to enter a fight.
5. An ancient Chinese musical instrument similar to the zither.
6. This means Zilu has made progress but he is not yet proficient. The Master's talks were often accompanied by background music. Commentators speculated that the tune Zilu played was too militant and noisy to Confucius' taste. The Master was therefore angry at him. When he found that his disciples began to look down on Zilu, he gave the latter his due so as not to embarrass him.

11.17

The Jisun Family was wealthier than the Duke of Zhou, yet Ranqiu helped them become even richer by increasing the levies. The Master said, "Ranqiu is no student of mine. Disciples, you may beat the drums and denounce him."

11.18

(The Master said,) "Gao Chai is dumb; Zeng Cen is slow; Zizhang goes to extremes and Zilu is rash."

11.19

The Master said, "Yan Hui's scholarship and character are near perfection, yet he is often impoverished. Zigong, not content with his lot, is engaged in trade and hoarding, and he is often right in his speculations."

11.20

Zizhang asked Confucius to define a good man. The Master answered, "He does not tread in the footsteps of others, nor does he gain entrance into the inner chamber."

11.21

The Master said, "I applaud someone who speaks sincerely. However, is he truly a man of honor, or is he simply putting on a dignified look?"

11.22

Zilu asked, "Should I practice at once what I've just learned?" The Master said, "Your father and elder brothers are still alive, how can you practice what you have just learned?"

When Ranyou asked the same question, the Master said, "Yes, you should."

(Commenting on this,) Gongxi Hua said, "I'm puzzled. They asked the same question, but got two different answers." Confucius said, "Ranyou usually holds himself back, so I urged him on. Zilu is too bold, so I tried to hold him back."

11.23

The Master was besieged at Kuang. Yan Hui fell behind. When he arrived, Confucius said, "I thought you were dead."

To which Yan Hui replied, "How would I dare to die when you, my Master, are still alive."

11.24

Ji Ziran[7] asked, "Could Zilu and Ranqiu be great ministers?"

The Master said, "I thought you would ask about someone else, never expecting you would mention Zilu and Ranqiu. A great minister should serve the ruler according to the Way. If he cannot do that, he should give up his post. All one can say is that Zilu and Ranqiu are capable ministers."

Ji Ziran then asked, "In that case, would they always do what they are told to do?" The Master said, "No, not to the extent of killing their father or ruler."

11.25

Zilu recommended Zigao to be the county magistrate of Bi. The Master said, "You are ruining someone else's son."

Zilu said, "In Bi, there are people, land and crops. Why must one study before he can be considered educated?"

The Master answered, "It is for such remarks that I dislike people who resort to sophistry."[8]

---

7. A member of the Jisun family.
8. Confucius disapproved of Zilu taking Zigao away from study.

Zilu, Zeng Xi, Ranyou and Gongxi Hua sat in attendance on Confucius. The Master said, "Because I am slightly older than you, no one is interested in my service. You often say, 'No one recognizes my worth!' If someone did recognize your worth, how would you serve him?"

Zilu answered without thinking, "Let's say a medium-sized state is hemmed in by several large states. It is harassed by troops from outside and suffer from famine at home. If I were sent there to govern, by the end of three years, I would have been able to imbue all the people with courage and set them on the right course."

The Master smiled. He then asked, "What about you, Ranyou?"

Ranyou replied, "Let's take a small state of sixty or seventy, or even fifty or sixty square *li*. If I were to govern it, by the end of three years, I would have made everyone prosperous. As for reviving the rituals and music, that would have to wait for a wise and honorable man to come along."

The Master asked further, "And you, Gongxi Hua, what would you do?"

"Not that I'm already capable, but I would be willing to learn. At times of ancestral worship and negotiations with foreign allies, I would dress up in ceremonial robe and cap, and serve as a minor protocol official."

"And what about you, Zeng Xi?" the Master asked.

Zeng Xi was coming to the end of a piece he was playing on the Se. He plucked the final note and laid the instrument down. Rising from his seat, he replied, "My idea is very different from theirs."

The Master said, "No harm in that. After all, each one of you is entitled to talk about your own aspirations."

Zeng Xi went on, "In late Spring, and everyone has put on spring clothes, I would, in the company of five or six adults and six or seven children, bathe in the Yi River and enjoy the breeze on the Rain Altar and sing our way home."

Heaving a deep sigh, the Master said, "I'm all for Zeng Xi!"

Zilu, Ranyou and Gongxi Hua then took their leave. Zeng Xi was the last to go. He asked the Master, "What do you think of my three fellow disciples' answers?"

The Master said, "Each spoke of his own aspiration, that's all."

"Why did you smile at Zilu?" Zeng Xi asked.

The Master said, "When governing a state, one must show deference for others. He was not at all modest, so I smiled at him."

"Was Ranyou really talking about governing a state?"

"Why can't a territory of sixty to seventy, or fifty to sixty, square *li* be called a state?"

"Then perhaps Gongxi Hua was not talking about the same matter?" Zeng Xi asked.

The Master said, "He referred to ancestral temples and meetings with allied states. What was he talking about then if not about governing a state? If he were to act only as a minor protocol official, who is going to take the role of a major official?"

Book 12

In this book Confucius explains his ideas to his disciples and others, the most important ones being those about the concept of humaneness (仁). The clearest definition of humaneness was to love other persons (12.22), expanded in his saying " Do not do unto others what you would not others do to you." (12.2) His other definition of humaneness (12.1)is much more complicated. The Master considered humaneness as restraining oneself and observing the rituals. People committed to humaneness must know how to control one's own action so that everything he does is in conformity with the rituals. That, of course, is a tall order.

In this connection, the ruler who would like to practice good governance must himself be upright. He must set an example for his officials and people (12.13). Confucius also considered gaining the trust of the people the top priority for the government, even more important than defense and sustenance (12.7).

12.1

Yan Hui asked about humaneness. The Master said, "To restrain oneself and observe the rituals constitute humaneness. Once you have done these, the world will consider you humane. However, the practice of humaneness depends on no one but yourself."

Yan Hui then asked, "What are the essentials of humaneness?"

The Master answered, "Do not look unless it is in accordance with the rituals, do not listen unless it is in accordance with the rituals, do not speak unless it is in accordance with the rituals, do not do anything that is not in accordance with the rituals."

Yan Hui said, "Though I am not intelligent, I shall stick to what you have just said."

12.2

Zhong Gong asked about humaneness. The Master said, "In public, act as if you were receiving an honored guest. While employing the services of the common people, act as if you were officiating at a major ceremony. Do not do to others what you do not wish others do to you. In this way, you will incur no bitter feelings against you whether in state or family affairs."

Zhong Gong said, "Though I am not intelligent, I shall follow what you have just said."

12.3

Sima Niu[1] asked about humaneness. The Master said, "A man of honor is cautious with his words."

Sima Niu asked, "Does that mean a man who is cautious with his words can be regarded as humane?"

The Master said, "How can a man not be cautious with his words when it is so difficult to turn his words into deeds?"

12.4

Sima Niu asked about being a man of honor. The Master said, "A man of honor is free from worries and fears."

Sima Niu asked, "Can one be called a man of honor simply because he is free from worries and fears?"

The Master said, "If one has a clear conscience, what has he to worry about and fear?"

---

1. Confucius' student.

12.5

Sima Niu complained, "Others have brothers, I alone have none."

Zixia said to him, "I have heard it said that life and death are decided by fate; wealth and rank decreed by Heaven. The man of honor is dedicated to his work, does nothing wrong and is respectful and polite to others. Thus, all people within the Four Seas are his brothers. Why, then, does he have to worry about not having any brothers?"

12.6

Zizhang asked about clear-sightedness. The Master said, "When one is not affected by slanders though they have been assiduously repeated, nor by false charges suddenly thrown at him, he can be said to be clear-sighted. More than that, he can be said to be far-sighted."

12.7

Zigong asked about government. The Master said, "The essentials of good government are abundance of food, plenty of arms and the trust of the people."

Zigong asked, "What if one of these three essentials had to be dispensed with, which one should it be?"

The Master said, "Arms."

"What if one of the remaining two had to be dispensed with, which one should it be?"

"Food," said the Master. "After all, since the beginning of time, no one has been able to escape the fate of death. But without the trust of the common people, the government would have nothing to sustain itself."

12.8

Ji Zicheng[2] said, "The important thing about a man of honor is his good intrinsic quality. (When he has good intrinsic quality,) what need is there for cultural refinement?"

---

2. Minister of Wei.

Zigong said, "What a pity that you should talk about a man of honor in such a way. A word once spoken cannot be overtaken even by a team of four horses. (To a man of honor,) cultural refinement is just as important as his intrinsic quality. The skin of a tiger or leopard would be no different from that of a dog or sheep once its colorful fur is shorn."[3]

12.9

Duke Ai (of Lu) asked Youruo, "We have had a poor harvest and I have not enough to cover my expenditures. What should I do?"

Youruo answered, "Why not introduce a tithe?" The Duke said, "I don't have enough to spend even if I double the rate, how could a tithe do?"

To which Youruo replied, "When the people have plenty, the sovereign will not be in want; when the people are in want, how can the sovereign have plenty?"

12.10

Zizhang asked how one could cultivate virtue and the ability to resolve doubts at times of confusion. The Master said, "Make it your guiding principle to be loyal and trustworthy and keep to the path of righteousness and you will be cultivating virtue. When you love a person, you want him to have a long life, but when you hate him, you want him to die. When you want him both to live and to die, that is confusion. 'If you did not love her for her riches, you must have forsaken her, for you have changed your mind'[4]."

12.11

Duke Jing (of Qi) asked Confucius about government. Confucius replied, "Let the sovereign be a sovereign, the subject a subject, the father a father, the son a son."

The Duke remarked, "Well said. If the sovereign did not act like

3. Fur is used here as a metaphor for cultural refinement.
4. From the *Book of Songs*.

a sovereign, the subject not like a subject, the father not like a father and the son not like a son, then even if there were plenty of grain, would I get my share?"

12.12

The Master said, "If there's anyone who can settle a litigation case on the basis of evidence provided by one party, Zilu is probably the one."

Zilu never puts off fulfilling his promise.[5]

12.13

The Master said, "In settling a lawsuit, I am little different from others. I feel it is best to do away with all lawsuits."

12.14

Zizhang asked about government. The Master said, "Never slacken your efforts at your post, show your loyalty when carrying out government orders."

12.15

The Master said, "The humane will not go astray for he is widely read and he keeps himself in line with the rituals."

12.16

The Master said, "A man of honor helps others to realize their best aims, but not their worst desires. A petty-minded man does the opposite."

---

5. Commentators find it hard to explain the logical connection between the two sentences. One explanation suggests that Zilu was quick-tempered and passed out judgment without hearing evidence by both parties to the litigation.

12.17

Ji Kangzi asked Confucius about government. Confucius said, "The word *zheng*[6] is a homonym of the word *zheng*[7]. If you set an example by being upright, who would dare to be otherwise?"

12.18

Ji Kangzi was disturbed by the large number of thieves. He asked Confucius for advice. Confucius said, "If you were not covetous, no one would commit burglary even if they were to be rewarded for doing so."

12.19

Ji Kangzi asked Confucius about government, "What do you think of killing those who do not follow the Way so as to move the people closer to those who follow the Way?"

Confucius answered, "In governing a state, what need is there for you to kill? If you govern the state well, the common people will naturally become good. The morality of the man of honor is like the wind. That of the petty man is like grass. When there is a wind, the grass is sure to bend in the direction the wind blows."

12.20

Zizhang asked, "What must a scholar do to become prestigious?"

The Master asked him, "What is your understanding of being prestigious?"

Zizhang answered, "To be well-known whether serving the state or the big family."

"But that is only being well-known and not prestigious. To win prestige, one must be upright and just, sensitive to others' words and observant of their moods and expressions, and always ready to give precedence to others. Such a person is sure to win prestige whether he serves the state or a big family. A well-known person may put on an appearance of being honorable, but acts to the contrary, and feels

---

6. 政 government.
7. 正 upright.

no qualms about it. Such a person can make himself well-known whatever he does, in or out of government."

12.21

Fan Chi accompanied Confucius on an outing to the Rain Altar. He said, "May I ask how one can cultivate virtue, clear up resentment against oneself and recognize foolishness?"

The Master answered, "What an excellent question! Isn't a person cultivating virtue when he places service before reward? Isn't he clearing up resentment when he criticizes his own mistakes rather than those of others? Isn't it foolishness when, in a sudden fit of anger, one neglects his own safety and even that of his parents?"

12.22

Fan Chi asked about humaneness. The Master said, "Love your fellow men."

He asked about wisdom. The Master said, "Know your fellow men." Seeing that Fan Chi failed to grasp his meaning, the Master added, "Promote the righteous and set them over the unrighteous. That can make the unrighteous righteous."

Fan Chi withdrew and went to see Zixia, saying, "Just now I asked the Master about wisdom and he said, 'Promote the righteous and set them over the unrighteous. That will make the unrighteous righteous.' What did he mean?"

Zixia said, "How rich the meaning of his words! When Shun took over the rein, he promoted Gao Yao from the ranks and by so doing, he kept those who were not humane at bay. When Tang took over the rein, he promoted Yi Yin from the ranks and, by so doing, kept those who were not humane at bay."

12.23

Zigong asked how one should treat his friends. The Master said, "Advise them in earnest and guide them tactfully, but if they refuse to listen, stop right there and do not lend yourself to rebuff."

12.24

Master Zeng said, "A man of honor makes friends through his learning and looks to friends for support in cultivating humaneness."

Book 13

Here Confucius continued to expound his theory of the importance of good government to the belittlement of farming, his reasoning being that with a good ruler the people would naturally be working hard for a good harvest(13.4). Passage 13.23 conveys an important message about harmony which has significant implications for our world today. A man of honor, Confucius noted, seeks harmony without sameness or identity of views. This was because he knew that his society was an hierarchical one and the best the different sections of the society should and could hope to achieve was some kind of harmony. China's present call for a harmonious society as well as a harmonious world where different states live in mutual respect and peaceful existence is in full accord with Confucius' ideal. This stand is based on the understanding that different cultures and national interests are a basic fact of life.

13.1

Zilu asked about government. The Master said, "Set an example yourself and the people will work hard." When asked to elaborate, the Master said, "Never slacken your efforts when carrying out this principle."

13.2

When serving as a steward for the Jisun Family, Zhong Gong asked how he should govern. The Master said, "Set an example for your subordinates; be lenient on minor offenses and promote those who are talented."

Zhong Gong asked, "How does one decide who among so many are talented and should be promoted?"

The Master answered, "Promote those you know are talented. Those who are talented but whom you fail to recognize will not be passed over by others."

13.3

Zilu asked, "Should the Duke of Wei let you administer his state, what is the first thing you would do?"

The Master said, "Use the names properly."

Zilu said, "Is that so! Aren't you being pedantic? Why must the names be used properly?"

The Master said, "How boorish you are! A man of honor would never offer an opinion on something he has no knowledge of. If things are not called by their proper names, one's argument cannot stand to reason. If one's argument cannot stand to reason, nothing can be accomplished. If nothing can be accomplished, the regulations and rituals as well as music will not flourish; if these do not flourish, punishment for crimes will not be appropriate; if punishment for crimes is not appropriate, the common people will have nothing to go by. Thus, when the man of honor uses a name, there must be a reason for it and what he says must be practicable. The man of honor is anything but casual with his words."[1]

---

1. There was an internecine struggle for power in the state of Wei during which both father and son tried to seize the rein. Since the distinctions between their status were blurred, Confucius advocated that the first measure to be taken should be the proper use of names.

13.4

Fan Chi asked the Master to teach him farming. The Master said, "I am not as good as an old farmer." When asked to be taught how to grow vegetables, he said, "I am not as good as a gardener."

After Fan Chi had left, the Master said, "Fan Chi is indeed a petty man! If those at the top observe the rituals, the common people will not dare show irreverence. If they are upright, the common people will not dare disobey. If they promote honesty, the common people will not dare to be deceitful. If they are able to do all this, the common people everywhere will flock to them with their babies strapped on their backs. What need is there for those at the top to learn farming?"

13.5

The Master said, "A person may be able to recite three hundred verses from the *Book of Songs* by heart and yet fails when given administrative responsibilities and proves incapable of using his own initiative when sent as emissary to foreign states. If such is the case, then what use is it for him to recite so much of this book?"

13.6

The Master said, "If a ruler is correct in his own behavior, then people will obey him without him giving any orders, but if he misbehaves, people will not obey him even if he issued orders."

13.7

The Master said, "In terms of government, the states of Lu and Wei are like brothers."[2]

---

2. When these two states were established, their founders were both sons of King Wen of Zhou.

13.8

Speaking of Prince Jing of Wei, the Master said, "He knew how to manage his property. When he began to have some means, he said, 'It is enough.' When he had a little more, he said, 'It is quite adequate.' When he became prosperous, he said, 'It is excellent!'"[3]

13.9

When Confucius went to the State of Wei, Ranyou drove the carriage for him. The Master remarked, "What a lot of people they have here!"

Ranyou asked, "What can be done with so many people?"

The Master said, "Help them prosper."

Ranyou asked, "When they have become prosperous, then what?"

The Master said, "Educate them."

13.10

The Master said, "If I were asked to serve In the government, I would have brought things to a satisfactory state in a year's time; and in three years, I should have achieved wonderful results."

13.11

The Master said, "How true is the saying that 'when good men have governed a state for a hundred years, then cruelty will have been banished and killings will have disappeared.'"

13.12

The Master said, "Even with a good king, it would still require an entire generation for his humane rule to prevail."

---

3. Prince Jing was a senior official of Wei. Among the ministers, embezzlement and extravagance were common. Therefore, Confucius praised Prince Jing's simple and frugal lifestyle.

13.13

The Master said, "If one is upright himself, he should have no difficulty in governance. If he is not upright, how can he correct others?"

13.14

Ranyou returned from the court. The Master asked, "Why so late?"

Ranyou replied, "There were state affairs to attend to."

The Master said, "They could only have been routine matters. Were they affairs of state, I would have heard about them, even though I am no longer in office."

13.15

Duke Ding of Lu asked, "Is there a single saying that can lead a state to prosperity?"

Confucius answered, "One cannot interpret it in such a simplistic way. There is a maxim which says 'it is difficult to be a sovereign, nor is it easy to be a minister.' If the sovereign realizes how difficult his role is, then won't that be almost a case of a single saying leading the state to prosperity?"

Duke Ding asked, "Is there a single saying that can lead a state to ruin?"

Confucius answered, "One cannot interpret it in such a simplistic way. There is a maxim which says that 'the one and only pleasure in being a ruler is that nobody dares disobey him.' If what he says is right and no one dares disobey him, isn't that a good thing? But if what he says is wrong and no one dares disobey him, will it not be almost a case of a single saying leading the state to ruin?"

13.16

The Governor of She asked about government. The Master answered, "Make those near you happy and those far away will flock to you."

13.17

On becoming the magistrate of Jufu, Zixia asked about government. The Master said, "Do not make haste. Do not covet small gains. Haste makes waste. Great tasks will not be accomplished if you covet small gains."

13.18

The Governor of She said to Confucius, "In my village there is an upright man who reported his father to the authorities for stealing a sheep."

Confucius said, "In my village, those who are upright are quite different. Fathers cover up for their sons, and sons cover up for their fathers. That is one example of being upright."[4]

13.19

Fan Chi asked about humaneness. The Master said, "Be courteous in daily life, conscientious at work and honest and sincere toward others. These are qualities which cannot be forsaken even if you go and live among the uncultivated tribes."

13.20

Zigong asked, "What kind of a person deserves to be called a scholar?"

The Master said, "A person who has a sense of shame and, when sent abroad by his ruler, accomplishes his mission, can be called a scholar."

"May I ask, what about the next down the scale?"

"Someone who is praised by his clan as a good son and, in his village, as being respectful to his elders."

"What about the next?"

"Someone who keeps his word and acts resolutely so that whatever he undertakes, he brings it to fruition, may make up the next, even if he is stubbornly petty-minded."

---

4. Confucius' ethics is based on the principle of paternal love and filial piety.

"What about those in government today?"

"Oh, they are so narrow-minded and of such limited capacity that they hardly count."

13.21

The Master said, "If one is unable to associate with those who follow the golden mean, then associate with those with ambition or those who are cautious. The former are enterprising while the latter will draw the line at certain kinds of behavior."

13.22

The Master said, "There is a saying among the southerners: 'A person who lacks constancy will not make a healer.' How true that is." "If one does not show constancy in virtue, one will someday suffer shame."[5] The Master commented, "For someone like that, there is no point in consulting the oracle."

13.23

The Master said, "A man of honor seeks harmony without identity of views; a petty-minded man seeks identity but not true harmony."

13.24

Zigong asked, "What do you think of a person who is liked by everyone in the village?"

The Master said, "That is not enough."

"What do you think of a person who is disliked by everyone in the village?"

"Not enough, either. It would be best if all the good people in his village liked him and all the bad people in his village disliked him."

---

5. From the *Book of Change*.

13.25

The Master said, "A man of honor is easy to serve but hard to please. If one tries to please him by means which are not in accord with the Way, he will not be pleased. When it comes to selecting someone for a job, he will base his choice on the person's capability and virtue. The petty-minded man is difficult to serve but easy to please. He will be pleased even if one goes against the Way. But when it comes to using such people, he is forever picking faults."

13.26

The Master said, "A man of honor is composed but not arrogant. A petty-minded man is arrogant but not composed."

13.27

The Master said, "Being staunch, resolute, modest and slow in speech makes one almost a man of honor."

13.28

Zilu asked, "What kind of a person can be called a scholar?"

The Master answered, "One who is respectful and cordial to others can be called a scholar. He is respectful to his friends and cordial to his brothers."

13.29

The Master said, "After being trained by a good man for seven years, the common people should be able to fight any battle."

13.30

The Master said, "To send people to war without giving them proper training is like throwing their lives away."

Book 14

Most of the comments Confucius made in this book concerned the politicians and other figures during and before his time. Readers will need some information about them to appreciate what he was talking about. One passage, however, is rather revealing about the Master himself. 14.2 says that "he who hankers after the comfort of home is not qualified to be a scholar." Confucius himself gave up the comfort of home and spent many years travelling from state to state to propagate his ideas, though without success.

14.1

Yuan Si asked about shame. The Master answered, "Whether or not the Way prevails in the state, to take office for pay would be shameful."

"Would someone be considered humane if he has overcome the faults of trying to be better than others, of bragging about himself, of bearing grudges against others and of being covetous?"

The Master answered, "It would be difficult to become such a person, but even then, I don't know if he can be considered humane."

14.2

The Master said, "He who seeks hankers after the comfort of home is not qualified to be a scholar."

14.3

The Master said, "When the Way prevails in a state, act in an upright way and speak boldly. When the Way does not prevail, act in an upright way but speak with caution."

14.4

The Master said, "A virtuous man is sure to be eloquent; but an eloquent man is not necessarily virtuous. A virtuous man is sure to be courageous; but a courageous man is not necessarily virtuous."

14.5

Nangong Kuok asked Confucius, "Yi was an excellent archer. Ao was skilled in sailing. Both met an untimely death. Yu and Ji, on the other hand, farmed the land. Both won the empire. (What conclusion can one draw from this?)" The Master gave no answer.

After Nantong Kuok had left, the Master said, "What a man of honor he is! How he upholds virtue!"

14.6

The Master said, "We have seen cases of a man of honor not being humane, but we have never seen a petty-minded man being humane."

14.7

The Master said, "Should we make no demands on those whom we love? Should we refrain from educating those we are loyal to?"

14.8

The Master said, "When it came to issuing an edict (in the state of Zheng), Pi Chen wrote the first draft, Shi Shu discussed the content and put forward suggestions, Zi Yu, master of protocol, revised it and Zi Chan polished it."[1]

---

1. All four were officials of Zheng.

14.9

Someone asked about Zi Chan. The Master said, "He was a generous man."

When asked about Zi Xi, he said, "Oh, that man, what can one say about him?"

Asked about Guan Hong, the Master remarked, "He was a real genius. He took three hundred households from the fief of the Bo family (in the city of Pain) and caused him to live on coarse grain for the rest of his life, yet the latter never complained."

14.10

The Master said, "To be poor and yet not resentful is difficult. To be rich and yet not arrogant is easy."

14.11

The Master said, "Meng Gung-ho[2] would be more than adequate serving as a steward of the Zhao or Wei family. But he would not be adequate serving as a minister even in small states like Tang or Due."

14.12

Zilu asked how to become an accomplished man.

The Master said, "If one is able to combine the wisdom of Zang Washing, the self-denial of Gung-ho, the courage of Bain Shaanxi and the skills of Ranqiu and, having done all this, he is further refined by the rituals and music, then he may be considered an accomplished man."

And he added, "But nowadays, an accomplished man may not possess all these qualities. He who can think of righteousness when gains come his way, who is ready to give up his life in the face of danger, and does not forget his promises when confronted with difficult circumstances, can be considered an accomplished man."

---

2. A minister of Lu.

14.13

The Master asked Gonging Jia about his master Gongs Wenzi[3] "Is it true that your master never spoke, laughed or took anything from others?"

Gonging Jia answered, "Whoever told you that got it entirely wrong. My master spoke only when it was necessary for him to do so, he laughed only when he was happy, and he took only what was his due. That is why people never got tired of him."

The Master said, "Is that so! Is it really so!"

14.14

The Master said, "Zang Washing made the Duke of Lu agree to appoint a member of his family to succeed him as the head of his fief. Someone said this was not coercion. I disagree."

14.15

The Master said, "Duke Wen of Jin was crafty and not upright. Duke Human of Qi was upright and not crafty."

14.16

Zilu said, "When Duke Human killed (his elder brother) Prince Jin, Zhao Hu committed suicide while Guan Hong did not. Wasn't he wanting in humaneness?"

The Master answered, "Duke Huan managed to forge an alliance with the feudal lords on several occasions. He did this without resort to force. He succeeded in doing this thanks to the advice of Guan Zhong. Such was the latter's humaneness, such was his humaneness."[4]

---

3. A minister of Wei.
4. Both Zhao Hu and Guan Zhong used to serve Prince Jin.

14.17

Zigong asked, "Wasn't Guan Zhong wanting in humaneness? When Duke Huan killed Prince Jiu, Guan Zhong (the latter's assistant) did not kill himself but lived on to become the Duke's chief minister."

The Master answered, "Guan Zhong assisted Duke Huan in gaining dominance over the feudal lords and in bringing order to all states under heaven. To this day, the common people continue to enjoy the benefits of his contribution. Were it not for Guan Zhong, we would still be wearing our hair unbound and folding our robes to the left.[5] Surely we would not want him to be like the common men who, in their petty loyalty to their ruler, committed suicide in a gully without anyone taking notice."

14.18

Zhuan, the steward of Gongshu Wenzi, was promoted to a ministerial post (of Wei) along with his master. On hearing this, the Master said, "Now, Wenzi deserves the title 'Wen' (of being cultured)."

14.19

The Master was speaking about the unprincipled course of Duke Ling of Wei when Kangzi asked, "If that's the case, why did he not lose his state?"

Confucius answered, "He had Zhong Shuyu in charge of foreign affairs, Zhu Tao of ancestral sacrifice and Wangsun Jia of military affairs. That being the case, how could he lose his state?"

14.20

The Master said, "He who speaks immodestly will find it hard to live up to his words."

---

5. Both styles were considered uncultured at the time.

14.21

Chen Chengzi killed Duke Jian (of Qi). After a ceremonial bath, Confucius went to the court of Lu and informed Duke Ai of the incident. "Chen Chengzi has slain his ruler," he said. "Please send an expeditionary force against him." The duke said, "Go and report to the Three Lords (Jisun, Zhongsun and Mengsun)."

(After he had left the court,) Confucius said, "Because I was once a minister, I dared not leave the case unreported. Yet the ruler asked me to 'report' to the Lords." He went and reported to the Three Lords, but they refused to take any action.

Confucius repeated, "Because I was once a minister, I dared not leave the case unreported."

14.22

Zilu asked about the way to serve a ruler. The Master said, "Do not deceive him (by feigning compliance). Rather, tell him the truth even if it offends him."

14.23

The Master said, "The man of honor reaches for higher things. The petty-minded man reaches for lower things."

14.24

The Master said, "In the past, people studied to improve themselves. Nowadays, they study to impress others."

14.25

Qu Boyu[6] sent a messenger to Confucius. After giving him a seat, Confucius asked, "How is your master?" The messenger answered, "My master tries to make fewer mistakes but has not yet succeeded."

After he left, the Master said repeatedly, "What an excellent messenger!"

---

6. A minister of Wei.

14.26

Confucius said, "While not in office, do not discuss official policies."

Zeng Zi commented, "The man of honor would never contemplate overstepping his position."

14.27

The Master said, "The man of honor considers it a disgrace to let his words outstrip his deeds."

14.28

The Master said, "The Way of the man of honor contains three principles, none of which I have been able to accomplish. Being humane, he has no worries; being wise, he is not confused and being courageous, he does not fear."

Zigong commented, "That is just a modest way by which the Master describes himself."

14.29

Zigong was talking about the faults of others. The Master said, "Zigong, are you so perfect yourself? I have no time for such prattle."

14.30

The Master said, "Worry not about others failing to appreciate you, worry about your own failings."

14.31

The Master said, "He who, without suspecting others or doubting his own credibility, is the first to be aware when others deceive him can be said to be a truly sagacious man."

14.32

Weisheng Mu asked Confucius, "Why are you rushing about so? Aren't you showing off your clever tongue?" Confucius answered, "I'm not so impertinent as to show off anything. I merely detest those with incorrigible stubbornness."

14.33

The Master said, "A steed which covers a thousand *li* a day is valued not for its strength but for its steadfastness."

14.34

Someone asked, "What do you think of the saying 'Repay injury with a good turn'?" The Master said, "How then are you going to repay a good turn? You repay an injury with justice. You repay a good turn with a good turn."

14.35

The Master said, "Alas, it seems that no one understands me." Zigong asked why this was so.

The Master said, "I bear no grudges against Heaven or men. I learn what is common knowledge but reach upward to the ways of Heaven. Perhaps Heaven alone understands me."

14.36

Gongbo Liao spoke ill of Zilu before Jisun. Zifu Jingbo[7] reported this to Confucius, saying, "My lord has been beguiled by Gongbo Liao, but I still have enough influence to have him killed and his corpse displayed on the market."

The Master said, "It is Heaven's will that decides whether the Way shall prevail or perish. What can Gongbo Liao do to me in the face of the will of Heaven?"

---

7. Confucius' disciple.

14.37

The Master said, "To some wise men (meaning the hermits), the highest form of wisdom is to shun the society. Next, to shun certain places. Next, to shun certain looks. And finally, to shun certain words. Seven men have accomplished this feat."

14.38

Zilu stayed for the night at the Stone Gate. The next morning, the gatekeeper asked him, "Where are you from?"

Zilu answered, "From Confucius."

The gatekeeper asked, "Is he the man who persists, knowing that his cause is hopeless?"

14.39

Once, the Master was playing the stone chimes in the state of Wei. A man carrying some baskets happened to pass by his door. He said, "The man playing the stone chimes seems to be deeply troubled in his mind."

Presently, he added, "How mean this stubborn sound is. If the world continues to ignore you, so be it. 'Where the river is deep, wade across; where it is shallow, lift your gown (to keep it dry).'[8]"

The Master said, "With such resolution, nothing is too difficult to handle."

14.40

Zizhang asked, "The *Book of Documents* says, 'King Gao Zong (of Shang Dynasty) remained in mourning for his father, and for three years he did not attend to state affairs.' What does that mean?"

The Master said, "Gao Zong was not the exception. People in ancient times all followed the same rule. When the sovereign passed away, his successor would not attend to state affairs for three years and all the officials would be under the command of the chief minister."

---

8. From the *Book of Songs*.

14.41

The Master said, "When those above observe the regulations and rituals, the common people will be easy to command."

14.42

Zilu asked about the man of honor. The Master said, "The man of honor cultivates himself to become respectable."

Zilu asked, "Is that all?"

"He cultivates himself and thereby brings peace and security to his fellowmen."

"Is that all?"

"He cultivates himself and thereby brings peace and security to the common people. This is hard to accomplish even for sage kings like Yao and Shun."

14.43

Yuan Xiang sat with his legs spread wide apart. The Master tapped him across the shin with his stick, saying, "You were defiant when you were young and you accomplished nothing when you were grown up. Now that you are old, you still refuse to die. You are what I call a pest."

14.44

A young man from Que Village came to see Confucius as a messenger. Someone asked the Master, "Is he going to make progress?" Confucius answered, "I have seen him take a seat and walk alongside his seniors. What interests him is not how to make progress but how to succeed quickly."[9]

---

9. In ancient China, only adults could be seated on a chair. By taking a seat, the young man had violated the rituals. Similarly, he was not supposed to walk alongside his seniors. He should have sat in the corner of the room and walked behind his seniors.

Book 15

There are many famous passages in this book, some of which have become maxims today. For instance, 15.9 says, " Those with public spirit and lofty ideas will not try to save their lives at the expense of humaneness. They will readily give up their lives for its sake." Many national heroes in Chinese history followed this dictum and gave their lives without the slightest hesitation. 15.12 says, "Sorrow awaits those who don't take a long view." 15.23 says , "A man of honor does not approve of a person simply because he expresses an opinion to his liking, nor does he reject an opinion because it is held by a person he dislikes." This, of course, is more easily said than done. How many times have we seen exactly the opposite? 15.24 " Do not do unto others what you would not others do to you" is perhaps the most famous and commonly quoted adage of Confucius. It can be compared a similar saying of Jesus. 15.30 says, "A mistake not corrected is a mistake indeed." How often have we seen people justifying or covering up their mistakes? And finally, 15.36 states, "Where humaneness is concerned, be not afraid to overtake your master."

15.1

When Duke Ling of Wei asked Confucius about military tactics, Confucius replied, "I have some knowledge about the regulations and rituals. As to military affairs, I have never studied them." He left Wei the next day.

15.2

While in the state of Chen, Confucius ran out of provisions. His disciples were so weakened that they could not stand on their feet. Zilu came to see Confucius and complained, "Does the man of honor have to suffer from hunger, too?" The Master answered, "When the man of honor bears hunger, he is undisturbed. But the petty-minded man throws caution to the wind whenever in want."

15.3

The Master said, "Zigong, do you think that I am a man with a wide range of knowledge and a good memory?" "Yes, I do, but isn't it so?" The Master said, "No. I have one single thread with which to bind together everything I know."

15.4

The Master said, "Zilu, how few are those who understand virtue!".

15.5

The Master said, "Nobody except Shun could govern so efficiently without exertion. What did he do? Nothing except sitting reverently in his royal seat facing south."

15.6

Zizhang asked how a man should conduct himself in order to get things done. The Master said, "If you speak with sincerity and trust and behave with honor and reverence, you will get things done even if you are living among backward tribes. However, if you do the contrary, will you get anything done even if you are among your neighbors? Wherever you are, at home or on the road, you should always keep in mind these principles, and you will get things done."

Zizhang had these words written on his sash.

15.7

The Master said, "How straight Shi Yu was! When the Way prevailed, he was as straight as an arrow. When the Way did not prevail, he remained the same. And what a man of honor Qu Boyu was! When the Way prevailed, he took office. When the Way did not prevail, he folded up and lived in seclusion."

15.8

The Master said, "To fail to advise a person who can benefit from it is to let that person go to waste. To advise a person who cannot benefit from it is to let your words go to waste. A wise man will waste neither man nor words."

15.9

The Master said, "Those with public spirit and lofty ideals will not try to save their lives at the expense of humaneness. They will readily give up their lives for its sake."

15.10

Zigong wanted to know how to practice humaneness. The Master said, "A craftsman must first sharpen his tools if he is to do his work well. Whichever state you happen to be in, serve the most virtuous of the ministers and befriend the most humane of the scholars."

15.11

Yan Yuan asked how a state should be governed. The Master said, "Use the calendar of Xia, ride in the carriage of Yin, and wear the ceremonial cap of Zhou. As for music, play the *Shao* and *Wu*, abandon the tunes of *Zheng* and stay away from the flatterers. The tunes of *Zheng* are lascivious and the flatterers are dangerous."

15.12

The Master said, "Sorrow awaits those who don't take a long view."

15.13

The Master said, "Alas! I have yet to meet a man who loves humaneness as he does beauty."

15.14

The Master said, "Zang Wenzhong[1] was an irresponsible official. He knew well that Liuxia Hui was a man of wisdom, yet he would not recommend him to an official post."

15.15

The Master said, "Require much of yourself and little of others, and you will stay away from ill will."

15.16

The Master said, "With those who never ask themselves, 'What should I do? What should I do?', I really don't know what I should do with them."

15.17

The Master said, "To mix with a crowd all day, handing out small favors, yet never touching on the subject of virtue—such a person is a hopeless case indeed."

15.18

The Master said, "The man of honor takes righteousness as his basic principle. He practices it by observing the rituals, gives it expression

---

1. A minister of Lu.

by being modest and brings it to fruition by being trustworthy. That, indeed, is what makes him a man of honor."

15.19

The Master said, "A man of honor fears his own insufficiencies, not the failure of others to understand him."

15.20

The Master said, "A man of honor worries that he might disappear from this world without leaving a name."

15.21

The Master said, "A man of honor sets demands on himself while a petty-minded man sets demands on others."

15.22

The Master said, "A man of honor is dignified but not contentious; he is sociable but not clannish."

15.23

The Master said, "A man of honor does not approve of a person because he expresses an opinion to his liking, nor does he reject an opinion because it is held by a person he dislikes."

15.24

Zigong asked, "Is there a single word which a person should take as his life-long motto?" The Master answered, "There is, and that word should be 'forbearance'. Do not do unto others what you would not others do unto you."

15.25

The Master said, "In dealing with the people around me, whom have I censured and whom have I praised? If I praised anyone, it was because his deeds had been put to test. The common people of the three dynasties (Xia, Shang and Zhou) followed the same principle, and that was why they kept to the Way."

15.26

The Master said, "I can still find certain ambiguities in historical documents. Those who had horses were supposed to allow others to use them. Such practices are extinct nowadays."

15.27

The Master said, "Being sweet-tongued is enough to forsake one's virtue. Lack of forbearance in small matters spoils great plans."

15.28

The Master said, "Be sure to look into a person's case when everyone dislikes him. The same when everyone seems to like him."

15.29

The Master said, "Man can enlarge the Way. The Way cannot enlarge man."

15.30

The Master said, "A mistake not corrected is a mistake indeed."

15.31

The Master said, "Occupied with thinking, I once spent days without eating and nights without sleep. My efforts turned out to be fruitless. I should have spent the time learning."

15.32

The Master said, "The man of honor seeks the Way. He is not concerned with making a living. Farm the land and you end up being hungry. Study and you end up being an official with earnings. The man of honor is worried about not finding the Way, rather than about living in poverty."

15.33

The Master said, "When a man has enough knowledge to attain office but fails to practice humaneness, even if he is in office, he is bound to lose his post. When a man has enough knowledge to attain office and has followed up by practicing humaneness, but fails to govern conscientiously, he will not win the respect of the common people. When a man has enough knowledge to attain office, has followed up with humaneness and has governed conscientiously, but fails to move the people with the spirit of the rituals, he still falls short of perfection."

15.34

The Master said, "The man of honor can be entrusted with great responsibilities but often fails in small matters. The petty-minded man can be entrusted with small matters but often fails in great responsibilities."

15.35

The Master said, "Humaneness is more vital to the common people than fire and water. I have seen people die in fire and water, but I have never seen anyone die by following the course of humaneness."

15.36

The Master said, "Where humaneness is concerned, be not afraid to overtake your master."

15.37

The Master said, "The man of honor is principled but he is not rigid about small matters."

15.38

The Master said, "When serving the ruler, attach great importance to the performance of your duties. How much you get for remuneration is secondary."

15.39

The Master said, "In teaching, I take disciples of all backgrounds without discrimination."

15.40

The Master said, "People who have different ideas about the Way need not consult each other."

15.41

The Master said, "Words are good enough as long as they can help get your ideas across."

15.42

The blind musician, Mian, called on Confucius. When he reached the steps, the Master said, "Watch your step." When they came to the mat, the Master said, "Here is the mat." When everyone was seated, the Master told Mian where the different people were seated.

After Mian left, Zizhang asked, "Is that the way to treat a musician?" The Master answered, "Yes, that is the way to help a blind musician."

Book 16

In passage 16.1, there is a phrase which has influenced Chinese psyche throughout the ages, i.e., "So long as there is even distribution, the common people will not feel the poverty." Many of the peasant uprisings in Chinese history erupted exactly because there was extravagance amidst extreme poverty. As the famous Tang Dynasty poet Du Fu wrote, "Behind the vermillion gates of the rich, meat and wine are left to rot, while on the road, lie the bones of the poor who have been frozen to death." 16.7 says, "The man of honor must guard against three dangers. When young, while the vital spirits are not yet settled, he should guard against lust. In the prime of life, during which the vital spirits are exuberant, he should guard against contentiousness. In old age, when the vital spirits are in decline, he should guard against greed." Even today, many Chinese intellectuals take this advice to their heart. 16.4 dwells on good and bad friends, 16.5 on good and harmful pleasures, and 16.6 on the kinds of mistakes one should try to avoid when attending those in power. Finally, 16.10 calls attention to the need for a man of honor to behave carefully.

16.1

The head of the Jisun Family was about to invade the principality of Zhuan Yu. Ranyou and Zilu, who were serving as stewards for the

Jisun Family, came to see Confucius and said to him, "Our lord is planning an operation against Zhuan Yu."

Confucius said, "Ranyou, isn't this your fault? Formerly, the King of Zhou delegated to Zhuan Yu the right to conduct the sacrifice to Dongmeng Mountain. Lying within Lu's boundary, the Mountain is crucial to Lu's security. What right has your lord to attack it?"

Ranyou said, "Our lord insists that we invade it. Neither of us favor the move."

Confucius said, "Ranyou, there is a saying of Zhou Ren[1] which goes: 'Those who are ready to play their role stay in the rank; those who are not had better get out.' What is the use of a helper to a blind man if he cannot support him when he trips or falls. Besides, what you said is incorrect. Is no one responsible when a tiger or a rhino escapes from its cage, or when tortoise shells and jade are damaged in the casket?"

Ranyou said, "Zhuan Yu is heavily fortified and it is close to Fei[2]. If we do not seize it now, it will surely become a threat to Jisun's descendants."

Confucius said, "Ranyou, a man of honor detests those who use pretexts to cover up their avarice. I have heard it said that what the head of a state or a noble family should worry about is not the lack of people but the uneven distribution of wealth, not poverty but the lack of stability. So long as there is even distribution, the common people will not feel the poverty. So long as there is stability, the common people will not worry about the scarcity of people. So long as there is stability, the government will not be threatened by disintegration. If, in such circumstances, the distant people still refuse to conform, you need only promote your own culture and virtue to attract them; once they have come, you should let them feel contented. However, you two, as stewards, have failed to attract distant people or preserve the state when it faces disintegration. Instead, you propose to use force within the state. I am afraid Jisun's troubles lie not in Zhuan Yu but within his palatial walls."

---

1. A historian.
2. A fief of the Jisun Family.

16.2

Confucius said, "When the Way prevails throughout the land, the Son of Heaven[3] has the final say on major issues like the rituals, music and military expenditures. When the Way does not prevail throughout the land, the rulers (of the various states) have the final say on such matters. When they have the final say, their rule will last no more than ten generations. When these prerogatives fall into the hands of their ministers, their rule will last no more than five generations. When these prerogatives fall into the hands of still lower officials, their rule will last no more than three generations. Thus, when the Way prevails throughout the land, decision-making does not rest with the ministers, nor do the common people ever comment on such matters."

16.3

Confucius said, "The ducal house of Lu has lost control of its revenues for five generations. The Three Lords, too, have lost control of this matter for four generations. For this reason, their descendants are going downhill."

16.4

Confucius said, "It is beneficial to make friends with three types of people: the upright, the trustworthy and the well-informed. It is harmful to make friends with three other types: the obsequious, the double-faced and the smooth-tongued."

16.5

Confucius said, "There are beneficial and harmful pleasures. To be restrained by music and rituals, to praise other people's virtues and to befriend worthy people—these are beneficial pleasures. To be soothed by licentious sounds, to idle away time and to indulge in banqueting—these are harmful pleasures."

---

3. The king of Zhou.

16.6

Confucius said, "There are three mistakes one has to watch out for when one is in attendance on the ruler. To speak before spoken to is being rash. Not to speak when spoken to is being evasive. To speak without observing the listener's facial expressions is being blind."

16.7

Confucius said, "The man of honor must guard against three dangers. When young, while the vital spirits are not yet settled, he should guard against lust. In the prime of life, during which the vital spirits are exuberant, he should guard against contentiousness. In old age, when the vital spirits are in decline, he should guard against greed."

16.8

Confucius said, "The man of honor holds three things in awe—the mandate of Heaven, people in high position and the words of sages. The petty-minded man, being ignorant of the mandate of Heaven, does not stand in awe of it. He treats people in high position with insolence and the words of the sages with disdain."

16.9

Confucius said, "Those who have innate knowledge are at the top of the scale. Those who study and learn come next. Those who study when faced with difficulties are lower still. Those common people who do not study even when faced with difficulties are the lowest."

16.10

Confucius said, "There are nine occasions which call for careful consideration by the man of honor: When using his eyes, is he seeing clearly? When using his ears, is he hearing distinctly? Regarding his countenance, does he look amiable? In his demeanor, does he appear reverent? When he speaks to people, is he sincere? In performing his duties, is he conscientious? When in doubt, does he seek answers from others? When in rage, does he consider its possible consequences. When faced with gain, does he ask himself whether it is his due."

16.11

Confucius said, "In pursuing goodness, I fear lagging behind. In avoiding vices, I stay away from them like I do boiling water. I have heard this said and seen it practiced. To live in seclusion in order to strengthen my aspiration; to follow what is righteous in order to realize the Way. I have heard this said, but I have never seen such a person."

16.12

"Duke Jing of Qi had a thousand chariots, but when he died, the people could not think of anything to praise him for. Bo Yi and Shu Qi starved to death at the foot of Shou-yang Mountain, but the people have been praising them ever since. Is this not proof of what we have just said?"

16.13

Chen Kang asked Confucius' son, Bo Yu, "Have you received any special coaching from the Master?"

He replied, "No. One day, my father was standing alone. As I hurried to cross the courtyard, he asked me, 'Have you studied the *Book of Songs?*' I answered, 'No.' He said, 'Unless you have studied it, you won't know how to speak properly.' I retired to study the *Book of Songs*. Another day, my father was again standing alone and as I hurried across the courtyard, he asked again, 'Have you studied the *Book of Rites?*' When I said no, he said, 'Unless you have studied it, you won't know how to behave properly.' I retired to study the *Book of Rites*. These were the two things I learned from him."

Chen Kang went away delighted, saying "I merely asked one question. However, I managed to learn three things: about the *Book of Songs*, about the *Book of Rites* and about how a man of honor keeps a distance from his son."

16.14

The ruler of a state calls his wife "my lady". When she talks to her husband, she calls herself "your little one". The people of the state refer to her as "the lord's lady". When going abroad, the ruler calls her "my little lord". People of other states also use the term "the lord's lady" when referring to her.

Book 17

The most controversial of Confucius' sayings in this book concerns his view on women. In 17.25, he said, "Women and the petty men are especially difficult to deal with. When you get too close to them, they become insolent, but if you keep them at a distance, they complain." Apologists tried to give a new twist to its meaning by changing the sentence's punctuation, but that would be untrue historically for, given the times Confucius lived in, he could not have looked upon women as equals, let alone cherishing the present feminist ideas. 17.3, which declares "only the intelligent elite and the ignorant masses will never change," is obviously politically incorrect. In 17.2, however, Confucius was right when he observed that human nature is alike for all humankind, only habits make people different. Today, we can add that culture, education and social background make people different.

Another passage (17.9) that might interest readers today is what Confucius said about poetry, as he is said to have edited the *Book of Songs*, the oldest collection of poems in Chinese history. Poems, he noted, "will enrich your imagination, enhance your power of observation, help you communicate with people and master the art of expressing grief. It will enable you to better serve your father and even your ruler. And you will learn the names of many birds and animals, plants and trees." Note that during Confucius' time, the language used at court was often filled with quotes from the *Book of Songs*.

17.1

Yang Huo wanted to see Confucius. When Confucius declined, Yang Huo sent him a steamed suckling pig.

Knowing that Yang was not at home, Confucius then went to his house to make a courtesy return call. On the way, the two happened to meet. Yang Huo said to Confucius, "Come now, I'll tell you something."

Then he went on, "Can one be considered humane when he hides his talents and allows his country to go astray? "I should say not." "Can one be considered wise who is eager to be in government and yet misses his opportunity to do so time and again?" "I should say not." "Days and months rush by, and the years do not wait for us."

Confucius then said, "All right, I'll take up office."[1]

17.2

The Master said, "What nature puts together, habit separates."

17.3

The Master said, "Only the intelligent elite and the ignorant masses will never change."

17.4

The Master went to Wu Cheng (where his student Ziyou was the county magistrate). There he heard the sound of music played on the *Qing* and someone singing. The Master broke into a smile and said, "Surely you don't need an ox-cleaver to kill a chicken."

Ziyou said, "Some time ago, I heard you say: 'When a man of honor is instructed in the Way, he will love his fellowmen; when a

---

1. Yang Huo was a steward of the Jisun Family. For years, Yang Huo was in control of the State of Lu through his power over the Jisun Family. Yang Huo would like to invite Confucius to serve him, but Confucius, being reluctant, was trying to avoid meeting him.

petty-minded man is instructed in the Way, it will be easier to command him.'"

The Master said, "My young friends, Ziyou is right. What I just said was merely a joke."

17.5

Gongshan Furao took the city of Fei and used it as his stronghold to stage a revolt (against the Jisun Family). He summoned Confucius to join him. The Master was inclined to do so.

Zilu was unhappy about this, saying, "We may have nowhere else to go, but must we really go and see Gongshan?"

The Master answered, "Do you think the man is summoning me for no reason at all? Should I get a post there, could I not establish a 'Zhou in the east'?"[2]

17.6

Zizhang asked Confucius about humaneness. Confucius said, "Whoever applies the five qualities to all under Heaven is humane."

"What are these five qualities?"

"Courtesy, tolerance, good faith, agility and generosity. Courtesy frees you from insults, tolerance wins the hearts of many, good faith secures the trust of others, agility leads to success and generosity gives one authority to use others."

17.7

When Bi Xi summoned Confucius, the Master intended to go.

Zilu said, "Master, I remember hearing from you that the man of honor does not associate with those who have committed evil. Now Bi Xi is entrenched in Zhongmo, ready to stage a revolt. Yet you are thinking of joining him. How can you justify yourself?"

Confucius said, "Indeed, I did say that, yet 'what is really hard

---

2. Confucius considered the Western Zhou Dynasty, especially during the reign of King Wu and his son assisted by his uncle Lord Zhou, as the ideal society. The state of Lu was to the east of the Zhou capital .

can never be worn thin; what is pure white can never be dyed black'[3]. Am I just a gourd good enough for decoration but is not edible?"[4]

17.8

The Master said, "Zilu, have you heard of the six qualities and their accompanying faults?"

"No, I have not."

Confucius said, "Sit down and I will tell you. To love humaneness but not learning may lead to foolishness. To love wisdom but not learning may lead to disorientation. To love good faith but not learning may lead you astray. To love forthrightness but not learning may lead to intolerance. To love courage but not learning may lead to insubordination. To love steadfastness but not learning may lead to recklessness."

17.9

The Master said, "My young friends, why do none of you study the *Book of Songs*? It will enrich your imagination, enhance your power of observation, help you communicate with people and master the art of expressing grief. It will enable you to better serve your father and even your ruler. And you will learn the names of many birds and animals, plants and trees."

17.10

The Master said to his son, Bo Yu, "Have you studied *Zhou Nan* and *Zhao Nan*?[5] A man who has not done so will be stonewalled and get nowhere in his life."

---

3. From the *Book of Songs*.
4. A figure of speech implying that Confucius hoped to secure an official position to carry out his political program.
5. *Zhou Nan* and *Zhao Nan* are the first two chapters of *Guo Feng* in the *Book of Songs*.

17.11

The Master said, "They talk of the rituals, but surely these are not limited to the ceremonial presentation of jade and silk. They talk of music, but surely it is not limited to the playing of bells and drums."

17.12

The Master said, "A coward who puts on a brave face is a petty man, like the thief who breaks in by digging a hole in the wall."

17.13

The Master said, "A person who never says no is the scourge of virtue."

17.14

The Master said, "One who spreads something based on hearsay casts virtue to the wind."

17.15

The Master said, "How can one collaborate with a rogue while serving the ruler? Before the rogue gets what he wants, he worries that he might not get it. After he has got it, he worries that he might lose it. Thus, in order to preserve it, he would be ready to go to extremes."

17.16

The Master said, "In ancient times, the common people had three faults, but even these faults have worsened today. The arrogant were reckless, but now they have become dissolute. The conceited were unpromising, but now they have become perverse. The foolish were straight, but now they have become deceptive."

17.17

The Master said, "A smooth tongue and an ingratiating manner are seldom the sign of being humane."

17.18

The Master said, "I detest purple replacing vermillion. I detest the pop tunes of Zheng replacing classical music. I detest the clever tongues subverting states and noble families."[6]

17.19

The Master said, "I no longer wish to say anything." Zigong said, "But if you don't say anything, what is there for us, your disciples, to transmit to others?" The Master said, "Has Heaven said anything? Yet the four seasons continue to run their course and the plants and animals keep growing. Has Heaven said anything?"

17.20

Ru Bei wanted to see Confucius, but the latter declined on grounds of illness. As soon as the messenger stepped out of the door, Confucius picked up his lute and began to sing, making sure that Ru Bei heard it.

17.21

Zaiwo said, "Three years is much too long for anyone to be in mourning for one's parents. If the man of honor does not practice the rituals for three years, they will surely be forgotten. If he does not play the music for three years, it will lose its tune. After the supply of old grain is exhausted and the new grain is in, and a new fire has been lit for the new year, that should be sufficient for the mourning period."

---

6. In ancient times, vermillion was considered the pure color. During the Spring and Autumn Period, some lords turned to dressing in purple. As a result, purple replaced vermillion as the pure color. Hence Confucius' reproach.

The Master asked, "Would you be at ease eating fine rice and wearing silk dresses during the three years' mourning?"

"Yes, I would," Zaiwo answered.

The Master said, "If you can be at ease doing all that, do as you please. A man of honor in mourning does not relish eating delicious food. He finds no pleasure in listening to music, nor comfort in his own home. That is why he has avoided these comforts. Since you seem to enjoy them, you might as well do what you please."

After Zaiwo left, the Master said, "How inhumane Zaiwo is. A child ceases to be nursed by his parents only after he is three years old. People everywhere under Heaven observe the custom of three years' mourning. Didn't Zaiwo enjoy three years of love and care from his parents?"

17.22

The Master said, "It is really intolerable for a person who has a full stomach not to use his brain all day. Why can't he play chess? Even that is better than being idle."

17.23

Zilu asked, "Does the man of honor value courage?" The Master said, "The man of honor considers justice the supreme good. Courage without justice would cause people to make trouble. It would turn the petty man to banditry."

17.24

Zigong asked, "Is there anything that the man of honor detests?" The Master answered, "Yes, there is. He detests those who go about publicizing the misdeeds of others. He detests those inferiors who slander their superiors. He detests those who possess courage but lack the spirit of the rituals. He detests those who are resolute but stubborn."

The Master then asked, "Zigong, is there anything you detest?" Zigong answered, "I detest those who consider themselves wise in plagiarizing other people's achievements, courageous in being rude, and forthright in exposing others' privacy."

17.25

The Master said, "Women and the petty men are especially difficult to deal with. They become insolent if you get too close to them, but if you keep them at a distance, they complain."

17.26

The Master said, "He who is still disliked at the age of forty has no hope left."

Book 18

During Confucius' time, there were quite a large number of people who stayed away from society due to dissatisfaction. Confucius was dissatisfied too, but he persisted in trying to become an official and reform the court with his teachings. While he failed to achieve his purpose, he never gave up his principles. He suffered many ridicules from these hermits, still he continued to pursue his own course. This book carries a good deal of such incidents and comments.

18.1

(King Zhou was very tyrannical.) Viscount Wei left him. Viscount Ji was condemned by him to be a slave. Bi Gan lost his life for remonstrating with him. Confucius said, "In these three men, the Shang (Yin) Dynasty found role models of humaneness."[1]

---

1. Viscount Wei was the elder step-brother of Zhou, the last King of the Shang Dynasty. Viscount Ji was Zhou's uncle. He tried to persuade Zhou to refrain from despotic rule. When the latter rejected his advice, he managed to save his life by feigning madness but was made a slave. Viscount Wei escaped. Bi Gan, Zhou's uncle and his prime minister, also remonstrated with the tyrant, who not only rejected his advice but also had his heart extracted.

18.2

Liuxia Hui was a judge who had been removed from office time and again. Someone said to him, "Why don't you go somewhere else?" He answered, "If, in the course of my service elsewhere, I refuse to change my way, would I be able to avoid the same fate? If I agreed to change my way, then there would be no need to leave the land of my parents."

18.3

Asked how he would treat Confucius, Duke Jing of Qi said, "I am unable to accord him the treatment that the Jisun Family received, so I shall place him somewhere between Jisun and Mengsun." "I am getting old," he explained, "I shall not be able to make use of his talents." Whereupon Confucius departed from Qi.

18.4

The State of Qi sent a group of sing-song girls to the State of Lu. Ji Huanzi[2] accepted them and, for many days afterwards, he stayed away from court. Whereupon Confucius departed from Lu.

18.5

Jie Yu, "the Madman of Chu," passed by Confucius' carriage, singing:
    "Oh phoenix, my phoenix!
    How your virtue has waned!
    The past is beyond retrieve,
    The future has yet to come.
    Worry not, worry not.
    There is nothing but danger
    For those in power today."

---

2. The Chief Minister of Lu.

Confucius stepped down, intending to speak to the "madman". But the man hurried off and Confucius never got to speak to him.[3]

18.6

Chang Ju and Jie Ni were ploughing the land together, yoked as a team. Walking past them, Confucius sent Zilu to ask them where the ford was.

Chang Ju asked, "Who is that driving the carriage?"

Zilu said, "It is Confucius."

"Then he must be the Confucius of Lu."

"He is."

"Then he should know where the ford is."[4]

Zilu then turned to Jie Ni.

Jie Ni asked, "Who are you ?"

"I'm Zilu."

"Then you must be a student of Confucius of Lu?"

Zilu answered, "I am."

"The world is now as turbulent as a river in spate. Who is there to change it? Rather than following a person who is trying to get away from one bad ruler to another, wouldn't it be better for you to follow someone who tries to get away from the bad world?" So saying, Jie Ni continued with his harrowing.

Zilu went back to report what he had heard to Confucius.

The Master was lost in thought. Afterwards, he said, "We cannot keep company only with birds and beasts. Who else should we have for company but people? Once the Way prevails in the world, you and I will have no need to try and change it."

---

3. Jie Yu was a hermit. In ancient times, it was believed that the phoenix would appear when the Way prevailed in the world. Jie Yu was comparing Confucius to a phoenix that refused to disappear even though the Way no longer prevailed. That's why he considered Confucius' virtue had waned.

4. Implying that since Confucius is much traveled, he should be familiar with the place's terrain.

18.7

When accompanying Confucius on his travels, Zilu fell behind. He met an old man carrying a stick and a hoe on his shoulder.

Zilu asked, "Have you seen my Master?"

To which the old man replied, "What kind of a master is he if he does not use his four limbs and cannot tell one kind of grain from another?" He then planted his stick in the ground and went on weeding.

Zilu stood there respectfully.

The old man invited Zilu to stay for the night, slaughtered a chicken and prepared some millet for his guest to whom he also introduced his two sons.

The next day, Zilu caught up with Confucius and told him his experience.

The Master said, "He must be a recluse", and sent his student back to look for the old man. But when Zilu returned to the site, the old man had already left.

Zilu commented, "It is not right to refuse to take office. We cannot abandon the mutual obligations between seniors and juniors, still less those between the ruler and his ministers. To keep one's virtue unsullied by withdrawing from the world is to cause confusion in the most fundamental human relationships. The man of honor takes office in order to perform his duty, knowing all along that the Way has not prevailed."

18.8

Bo Yi, Shu Qi, Yu Zhong, Yi Yi, Zhu Zhang, Liuxia Hui and Shao Lian were men who eventually withdrew from mundane affairs. The Master said, "Bo Yi and Shu Qi would not compromise their aspirations, nor disgrace their integrity. Liuxia Hui and Shao Lian compromised their aspirations and suffered disgrace. But their words were consistent with their status and their behavior prudent. That is all one can say about them. Yu Zhong and Yi Yi led the life of a recluse and spoke their minds freely. They kept their character unsullied and showed sound judgment in accepting their dismissal. I am different from them in that I don't think there is any rigid rule as to what one should or should not do."

18.9

The master musician, Zhi, left for Qi. The musician for the second course, Gan, left for Chu. The musician for the third course, Liao, left for Cai; the musician for the fourth course, Que, left for Qin. The drummer, Fan Shu, went to live in seclusion by the Yellow River. The player of the hand drum, Wu, settled along the Han River. The master musician's deputy, Yang, and player of the chime bells, Xiang, settled by the sea.[5]

18.10

The Duke of Zhou told (his son) the Duke of Lu, "The man of honor does not neglect his relatives, nor would he let his ministers complain of not having his trust. Unless they make serious mistakes, those who have served for long years should not be dismissed. Do not demand perfection from any individual."

18.11

There were eight great scholars during the Zhou Dynasty: Bo Da, Bo Kuo, Zhong Tu, Zhong Hu, Shu Ye, Shu Xia, Ji Sui and Ji Gua.

---

5. When the rituals collapsed in the state of Lu and ritual music was abandoned, the musicians each went their own way. In ancient times, the rulers had their meals to the accompaniment of music and each musician would play for a specific course of food. Hence the titles "the musician for the second course", "the musician for the third course", and so on.

Book 19

All the passages in this book were the sayings of Confucius' disciples. Here it is interesting to note that after Confucius' death, several people tried to belittle the Master in front of his disciple Zigong, even telling him to his face that he was greater than Confucius. Zigong, however, resolutely rebuffed them, comparing his Master to a mansion with towering walls whose magnificence cannot be seen from the outside, to the sun and moon whose greatness would not be impaired in the least despite the eclipses and to the sky which cannot be reached using a ladder (19.23, 19.24 and 19.25).

19.1

Zizhang said, "What more could be asked of a scholar who is ready to lay down his life in the face of danger, who keeps righteousness in mind when there's opportunity for gain, and who shows reverence while performing sacrificial ceremonies and who shows sorrow at mourning."

19.2

Zizhang said, "If a man is not steadfast in acting virtuously and forsakes his own beliefs, what does it matter whether he is alive or dead?"

19.3

One of Zixia's disciples asked Zizhang about making friends. Zizhang asked, "What has your master told you?"

The student answered, "Be friendly with good people and spurn those who are not."

Zizhang said, "That's not what I was taught. I was taught that the man of honor respects the virtuous and tolerates the ordinary. He lauds the wise while sympathizing with the mediocre. If I am a truly virtuous man, why should I be intolerant of others? If I am not, then the others will spurn me, then how can I spurn them?"

19.4

Zixia said, "Even minor arts have their worth, but the man of honor with a long journey ahead does not engage in them for fear of being bogged down."

19.5

Zixia said, "He who is aware of the need to learn every day and reviews each month what he has learnt is truly fond of learning."

19.6

Zixia said, "Learn extensively, hold fast to your purpose and interest, pose questions in earnest and reflect on issues at hand, then humaneness is within reach."

19.7

Zixia said, "The artisans master their crafts by living in their workshops. The man of honor arrives at his Way through learning."

19.8

Zixia said, "The petty-minded man tries his best to cover up his errors."

19.9

Zixia said, "The man of honor leaves people with three different impressions: From a distance, he looks solemn; when close at hand, he is cordial; when he speaks, it is with a firm tone."

19.10

Zixia said, "The man of honor has first to win the trust of the common people before he can make them work. Otherwise, they will feel abused. He has first to win the confidence of the ruler before he can remonstrate with him, for without this confidence, the ruler might take it as an insult."

19.11

Zixia said, "One must not step out of bounds on matters concerning virtue. Transgressions on small matters are permissible."

19.12

Ziyou said, "The disciples and followers of Zixia can manage such trifles as sweeping and cleaning, and escorting and sending off guests. But when it comes to the basics[1], they have no idea. How can that be?"

When Zixia heard this, he said, "Alas, Ziyou has got it wrong. In teaching the Way of a man of honor, what is to be taught first and what last? It is like the classification of plants, which can only be done according to the specific features of each. How can one distort the way of the man of honor? It is probably a sage who alone can teach his disciples in the proper order from beginning to end."

19.13

Zixia said, "A good scholar should make a good official, a good official should continue with his studies."

---

1. The rituals and music.

19.14

Ziyou said, "When in mourning, one should not go beyond expressing grief."

19.15

Ziyou said, "My friend Zizhang is a rare talent. Still, he has not yet attained humaneness."

19.16

Master Zeng said, "Zizhang is such a great scholar that it is difficult to arrive at humaneness together with him."

19.17

Master Zeng said, "I once heard the Master say that it is only when mourning for one's parents does one fully reveal his emotions."

19.18

Master Zeng said, "I once heard my Master say, one may emulate Meng Zhuangzi's filial piety, but it will be difficult to follow his example of not removing his father's ministers or changing his policies."

19.19

The Mengsun family appointed Yang Fu judge. Yang Fu sought Master Zeng's advice. The latter said, "Those in authority have lost the Way and the common people have long lost faith in them and become disorganized. If you succeed in extracting the truth from the criminals, have pity on them and do not pat yourself on the back."

19.20

Zigong said, " Zhou (of Shang Dynasty) may not have been as bad a ruler as he was said to be. That is why those in authority are afraid of landing on the wrong side of history. Once they are in that situation, all the dirt of the world will be thrown on them."

19.21

Zigong said, "The man of honor's mistakes are like the eclipses of the sun and the moon. When he makes a mistake, everyone will notice it. When he corrects his mistake, he will be looked up to all the more."

19.22

Gongsun Chao of Wei asked Zigong from whom did Confucius acquire his learning.

Zigong answered, "The Way of King Wen and King Wu (of the Zhou Dynasty) is not lost. It can be found among the people. The virtuous grasps its essence while the mediocre grasps the details. The Way is omnipresent. Where can't my Master learn? Where is the need for him to have one specific teacher?"

19.23

Shusun Wushu2 told his fellow officials in court, "Zigong is wiser than his Master."

Zifu Jingbo3 reported this observation to Zigong.

Zigong said, "Let's take the outside wall of a house as a metaphor. My wall is at shoulder height, so that the fine architecture inside can be seen from without. My Master's wall is several scores of feet high. If one is unable to find the entrance, he cannot see the magnificence of the ancestral temples and the splendor of the mansions within. Since those who can find the entrance are at best a few, is it not understandable that your master should have spoken thus?"

---

2. A minister of Lu.
3. Also a minister of Lu.

19.24

Shusun Wushu slandered Confucius. Zigong said, "It will make no difference. Confucius is above slander. Other virtuous men are like low hills that can be surmounted. But Confucius is like the sun and the moon that are insurmountable. Even if someone wanted to alienate himself from them, that would not harm the sun and the moon one bit. It would only serve to show that he did not know his own measure."

19.25

Chen Ziqin said to Zigong, "Surely you are being respectful to Confucius. Do you really think he is superior to you?"

Zigong said, "A single utterance is enough to judge whether a man is wise or foolish. That is why one must be careful with his words. The Master cannot be equaled just as the sky cannot be reached by climbing a ladder. Were the Master to become the head of a state or of a noble family, he would have been able to accomplish what is described in the saying; 'He only has to raise them and they will stand up, to guide them and they will walk, to grant them peace and they will turn to him, to motivate them and they will work in harmony.' My Master deserves honor while alive. When he dies, he deserves to be mourned. How can he be equaled?"

Book 20

This last book is different from the others in that there are only three passages. The first one is rather long and the speakers were the ancient kings Yao and Shun, as well as King Tang of the Shang Dynasty and King Wu of Zhou Dynasty. All of them advised their successors on how to rule, stressing the importance of benefiting the people. The second and third passages are quotes from Confucius. In the second passage (20.2), the Master told his disciple Zizhang to respect the five virtues and spurn the four evils. Admonishment of this type is quite common even in today's official pronouncements.

20.1

Yao said, "Oh, Shun, it is ordained by Heaven that the succession is to fall on you. You are to follow the middle way. If the multitude within the Four Seas should ever fall into poverty and misery, the blessing which Heaven bestowed on you will end forever."

Shun spoke the same words to Yu when proclaiming him the successor.

King Tang of Shang said, "I, Lü, the little one, venture to offer a black bull and make this declaration to you, the great Lord of Heaven: I dare not pardon those who have transgressed. Nor do I conceal the performance of my ministers, on whom you have already passed judgment. If I am found guilty, please do not let the people of the ten thousand fiefs suffer because of me; if the people of the ten thousand fiefs transgress, the guilt is mine alone."

During the Zhou Dynasty, a great number of people were made fiefs and the good people became prosperous. King Wu said, "Although I have many relatives, I prefer the virtuous. If the common people make mistakes, the blame is on me alone."

Unify weights and measures, standardize laws and regulations, and re-establish official posts which have been abolished, then government orders will be carried out throughout the country. Restore states which have been destroyed, revive lineages of big families which have become extinct, promote talents who have withdrawn from society and the hearts of all the common people under Heaven will turn to you.

Great attention should be paid to the common people's food supply and funeral and sacrificial rituals.

Tolerance gains the support of the multitude. Good faith wins the trust of the common people. Industriousness leads to success. Impartiality brings joy.

20.2

Zizhang asked Confucius, "How does one qualify for a government official?"

The Master said, "The qualifications are: respect the five virtues and spurn the four evils."

"What do you mean by the five virtues?" asked Zizhang.

The Master answered, "The man of honor is generous without excesses. He makes people work without causing them to complain. He is ambitious without being greedy. He is self-possessed without being arrogant. He is awe-inspiring without being fierce."

"What do you mean by being generous without excesses?" asked Zizhang.

The Master answered, "If you let the common people do what is beneficial for them, isn't it being generous without excesses? If you make people work on tasks they are capable of accomplishing, who will complain? If your ambition is to attain humaneness, there would be no place for greediness. The man of honor puts the many on a par with the few, the high on a par with the low and dares not to be negligent, isn't that being self-possessed without being arrogant? The man of honor dresses properly and looks dignified, his solemnity causing fear. Isn't he awe-inspiring without being fierce?"

Zizhang asked, "What do you mean by the four evils then?"

The Master answered, "To impose the death penalty without first educating the people amounts to cruelty. To demand achievement without prior requirements amounts to tyranny. To suddenly impose a deadline on a job without previous warning amounts to theft. To act miserly when it comes to giving amounts to stinginess."

20.3

Confucius said, "He who doesn't know his destiny will never become a man of honor. He who doesn't know the rituals will never become established. He who cannot judge the words of others will never be able to really know those who uttered them."

Confucius and Chinese Historiography

In ancient China, many records concerning the preservation of rites and music were lost in wars between feuding states. The contributions of Confucius to Chinese and World history lie not just in his collecting and editing of many lost rites of the Xia, Shang, and Zhou periods.

Certain officials were designated as responsible for the recording of history. Speeches were recorded by officials called *zuoshi*, while events were recorded by officials called *youshi*. The collection of ancient texts is a document of politics and history in the style of remark-keeping (i.e. prayers, instructions, oaths, admonitions). Some remarks became the record of the times, and some were taken down by later generations according to their recollections. The main such collections were known as *The Book of Xia*, *The Book of Zhou*, and *The Book of Shang*. These books were disorganized and unknown to most people until Confucius collected and edited them.

Confucius revised and edited these political documents into what later generations called the *Collection of Ancient Texts*. It included 50 essays and later developed into 100 essays with commentary included in each section. The records were arranged chronologically, from Yao and Shun to Mu, king of Qi in the Spring and Autumn period. By the Period of the Warring States, The Book of Yao, Prayers of Gao Tao, Remarks of Yu and others were added by later scholars. All of them represent Confucian thought. He taught them to his disciples and even practiced them personally, especially during the time after he came back to Lu. Confucius classified the rites into eight categories: Mourning, sacrifice, archery, provincial examinations, come-of-age ceremony, marriage, and official appointments. Under each main category, there were many sub categories.

In the early years of the Western Zhou, the king of Zhou offered feudal lands to his subjects. Those who had helped in establishing the kingdom were honored with the title of Marquis. Among the ducal states, officials were called senior officials. Below the senior officials were family subjects and commoners. As for slave owners and nobles, they had many titles equivalent to duke, marquis, earl, and viscount. The hierarchical system in Zhou Dynasty and the ducal states was so strict that no one was permitted to bypass or change it. But in the Spring and Autumn Period, with the development of economy, private land ownership was gradually replacing public land ownership and the old system of rites had crumbled in the political whirlwind. In the early years of Spring and Autumn Period, Duke Huan of Qi united the country and later, Duke Wen of Jin forced the king to help him control the various marquises, after which he became a ruler.

The State of Chu, which was ruled by an earl, also came to seek power in central China. The states of Wu and Yue regarded as inferior foreigners, nevertheless prospered in the late years of Spring and Autumn Period. At the time, the preservation of ancient rites and music had crumbled as various states struggled for power; senior officials competed for influence amid the various states, officials assassinated kings and sons killed fathers as the hierarchy was broken. Under such circumstances, Confucius was determined, once he became engaged in politics, to make every endeavor to bring back the best time of the Western Zhou. This aspiration remained heavy in his heart, and he couldn't forget it for a moment even as he was forced for political reasons to move from one state to another. But his ideas were becoming increasingly obsolete as Chinese society grew more complex.

To Confucius, the early years of the Western Zhou was the best time, therefore it became his starting point for the changes he wished to undertake in society. He set out to compile the first systematic chronology of China, the Spring and Autumn Annals, which begin with records of 722 BC (the beginning year of Duke Yin of Lu) and end in 481 BC (the 14th year in the reign of Duke Ai of Lu), covering a span of more than 240 years of history in the early years of Eastern Zhou. The Spring and Autumn Annals represented the embodiment of Confucius' views. He strongly opposed those who struggled for power and disrespected their superiors to start a rebellion.

As the first chronological history of China, The Spring and Autumn Annals recorded events according to the order of year, month and day, which was helpful for systematic understanding of their inter-relations. The Annals set an example for other his-torical books as a book that serves the political purpose of a class. It was the first history book independently edited by an individual in China. The Spring and Autumn Annals put emphasis on current history and society though it recorded ancient events, which enlightened the fol-lowers of Confucius.

The series of blows Confucius suffered in his later years: the sud-den death of his son, wife, and favorite disciple, took their toll on his health. He became physically weak. He was disgusted by political intrigue such as Ji Sun Shi's new system of field taxation in the state of Lu, and Chen Heng murdering his sovereign in the State of Qi. Trapped in failure and unable to find a way out, Confucius became more nostalgic for ancient times. In his dreams, he met the Duke of Zhou and talked with him about restoring the ancient rites. But even hope faded from his dreams and the Duke of Zhou no longer ap-peared before him. One night, Confucius had a dream that left him shaken: so much so that he woke before dawn, and, supported by his walking stick, leaned against his door. When Zi Gong came to see him, Confucius said, "Why are you so late to see me?" And then he recited a poem:

Fallen Mount Tai!
Collapsed the great beam!
Withered away the great sage!

At this, Zi Gong said, "If Mount Tai has fallen, how can people survive? If the beam has collapsed, how can the house stand? If the sage has withered away, who can lead us?" With these words, he supported Confucius back inside his house. Back in bed, Confucius told Zi Gong about his dream in which he was together with his ancestors. Confucius died in 479 B.C., in the 16th year of the reign of Duke Ai of Lu. He was buried near the bank of the Sishui River, more than one mile north of Lu City.

His disciples built a traditional, elliptical grave. Many disciples who came to mourn brought with them saplings to plant around the grave. Eventually these grew into a forest called by later generations the "Forest of Confucius." The place where Confucius' disciples lived while guarding the grave for three years was called "Kong Li" (Confucius' home). Through years of development, the "Forest of Confucius" covers an area of more than one square kilometer.

Confucius had been loyal to his sovereign. After Confucius' death, Duke Ai of Lu wrote of his passing: "How cruel is Heaven!" Confucius had stated "I preach but I don't write." Throughout his life, except for his commentary on the Chinese classics records, he seldom wrote anything. It was up to his disciples to collect and compile his remarks. These became The Analects, which is known worldwide as being the core book of Confucian thought and is one of the most important books in the Chinese philosophical canon.

After his death, Confucius was honored with numerous posthumous titles by emperors in differ-ent dynasties such as "Supreme Sage and Foremost Teacher," "Great Perfect Sage, Most Holy Culture Spreading King," "A Great Sage in this Fateful World, and an Ideal Teacher for Myriads of Years" to mention just a few. He has been the greatest ancient Chinese sage for more than 2,000 years. Confucianism, created by and named after Confucius, has been the most important part of Chinese traditional culture after so many years of inheritance, innovation and development. When Emperor Qianlong undertook a pilgrimage to Qufu in the thirteenth year of his reign (1748), he wrote a poem on that occasion, entitled "A Poem Composed Drunk When Paying Homage at Confucius' Mausoleum":

"Your teaching will long benefit the generations. Mount Tai will stand as witness. And this is true."

Afterword

In the late 1990s, I began my new translation of *The Analects* in the beautiful seaside city of Qinghuangdao. I had time to add to my understanding of the original text by reading up on all the relevant academic works available to me. This process of deepening and expanding continued for over a decade during which I re-edited my own translation many times.

A word of explanation is needed as to why I describe my book as a "new" translation. It is new because it benefits from the latest research materials on *The Analects* published by Chinese academia.

I want specially to thank my wife Zhang Qingnian for her unflinching support and encouragement. She is the translation's first reader and her criticisms and suggestions did much to improve its faithfulness and readability.

Lin Wusun

About the Translator

Wusun Lin is one of China's foremost translators. He has authored and translated numerous publications on Chinese literature, philosophy, history, and culture. During a career spanning more than five decades, Professor Lin has maintained an intense interest in Chinese and Western thought and has been a key figure in the promotion of Chinese literature and culture to a Western audience. He has studied in China, India, and the United States.

His translated works cover a wide range of topics, from international affairs, politics, and economics to philosophy, religion and culture, including Sun Tzu's *The Art of War*, Sun Bin's *The Art of War*, Xiong Kuangkai's *International Situation and Security Strategy*; *Riverside Talks—A Friendly Dialogue between an Atheist and a Christian* by Luis Palau and Zhao Qizheng, and *Shanghai Pudong Miracle: A Case Study of China's Fasttrack Economy* by Zhao Qizheng and Shao Yudong.

Professor Lin has served as Executive Vice-President of the Translators Association of China; Editor-in-Chief of Chinese Translation Journal, and Chair of the Chinese National Committee for the Accreditation of Senior Translators. He has also served as Adjunct Professor of the School of Journalism and Communications and Tsinghua University, Beijing, and Professor Modern Chinese Thought at the University of Chicago-sponsored Institute for the International Education of Students in Beijing.

Made in the USA
Charleston, SC
13 July 2013